ANNIE'S FARMHOUSE KITCHEN

ANNIE'S FARMHOUSE KITCHEN

Seasonal menus *with* a French heart

———————

ANNIE SMITHERS

with illustrations by
ROBIN COWCHER

hardie grant books

INTRODUCTION

I grew up in the 1970s in the bucolic world of a small acreage and luxurious dinner parties thrown by my parents. My mother, an English literature teacher, was a woman of excellent cooking skills and had a fine intellect devoted to words and books (Julia Child, Alice Waters and Simone Beck featured strongly in my childhood). People often remarked that Mum was such a good cook that she should open a little restaurant, and the memories of this time have had a significant impact on how I cook and how I live my life.

Perhaps it was inevitable that I would open a restaurant with all the bells and whistles, but in the end I decided this was not the right fit for me, and instead opened a tiny country restaurant that offers a menu du jour put together with my acre of garden that produces up to ninety per cent of my fruit and vegetable needs. I realise that I am absolutely living the dream, or at least my interpretation of it.

Every week at du Fermier (my little restaurant) we construct a different three or four course menu around what is coming from the garden, what the weather is like and where my mood is. The food is unashamedly French farmhouse as it's a style of cooking that has vast possibilities,

yet a familiarity that is truly comforting. I also conduct cooking classes in my home kitchen (with my animals watching on) to an ever-increasing circle of eager students. I listen carefully to their chatter, and it seems that what a lot of home cooks hanker for is certainty. They want a menu that goes together structurally, that is achievable in the domestic kitchen, and pushes them but doesn't leave them stressed and anxious as their guests arrive.

The menus at du Fermier follow a particular pattern. I always begin with a preparation day to start the elements that need time, such as slow-cooked braises and stocks. Then each service day I arrive about three hours before the customers and quietly go about preparing lunch for thirty. When it came to writing this book, it made sense to organise the recipes in planned menus, to enable you to present a beautiful meal to your family and friends. It may well take you more than three hours to get ready for eight people, but you must remember that I have honed this craft over thirty years.

Every recipe in this book is perfectly fine served as a stand-alone dish, but what I hope to do is give you the confidence to cook a well-balanced multi-course menu similar to those that grace my restaurant tables. As apprentices, we were taught how to assemble our 'mise en place', which literally means 'put in place'. We were also encouraged to write flow charts of how our preparation tasks are best ordered, so at the end of each menu you'll find a timeline, suggesting the best way to cook and serve each complete menu. Sometimes the instructions will differ slightly from those in the recipes, which I have written to be stand alone.

A friendly word of warning: not all recipes work the first time for everybody. I couldn't begin to count the number of curious results I have had over the last thirty years. Good cooking takes practice, sometimes lots of practice, but don't be frightened to try a particular dish or skill over and over again. Be kind to yourself; analyse what has gone wrong and you will learn to do it better next time. I am also not averse to a spot of repetition. The more you cook the more you see that classic techniques and combinations can be adapted and used over and over again. They are classics because they work. For instance, I have wholeheartedly adopted the French love of fruit and puff pastry, a blissful combination that works throughout the year – just change the fruit and change the sauce to reflect the seasonality of the dish.

When I'm not at the restaurant, I'm at home on my little farm with my animals. Firstly, there is Kitten – a cat who, through tragic circumstances, never got a proper name. He is my companion animal par excellence: an affable creature who captures the hearts of even the most hostile cat haters when they visit. His antics, his quiet presence and his day-to-day existence beside mine always make me smile. He is joined on the farm by the big cat, Fenn, and Tommy the Cairn Terrier. They coexist reasonably peacefully with geese and chickens, and together we form a noisy rabble that is home. A home where the traditions of honest, unfussy, delicious food are king, and my friends, family and creatures are more than happy to be their subjects.

I hope the recipes in this book inspire you to cook for the people in your kingdom and give you that wonderful glow of achievement that comes from pushing yourself a little and sharing something you've made yourself with those you love the most.

AUTUMN
(FALL)

AUTUMN

Each season has its own charm, its own pace. And autumn seems to cover the most ground. Starting with intense, residual heat from summer, it can quickly throw a cruel frost at you, only to recover and bring seemingly endless Indian summer days. But the days inexorably become shorter and the mornings colder and you know that the seasons are on the shift. It seems, too, to be the most productive of seasons. The abundance of vegetables and the procession of fruit, starting with the apples and plums and then meandering through quince, pears, crab apples and medlars, give the cook a rich pool of inspiration. Traditionally on the farm it's the time to lay down food for the winter, but this is something we no longer have to do to survive. Yet I find myself stewing, preserving and rendering fat to keep some reminders of the warmth, for when the cold descends there seems to be an interminable wait for the bounty of autumn to come again.

Autumn is also the season to delight in the birds born in spring, fattened over the summer and ready for the table. We forget in the age of supermarkets that all types of produce still have a definitive season and a suitability for the time of year. Sometimes we forget to listen to the seasons, but when you eat mushrooms and chestnuts on a late-autumn evening, seasonal food suddenly makes perfect sense.

I spend a lot of time in the yard in the autumn as it's the busiest time for harvesting. But the simple, quiet joy of my autumn harvesting is often shattered. There is never any warning; just a sudden, searing pain followed by the realisation that it is just Kitten.

There he is, on my shoulder wanting to see what I'm doing, all the while rhythmically pushing his claws in and out of my skin. Kitten's desire to be close to me is touching, but his determination to be on my shoulder brings mixed feelings. He is a very large cat. Now, when I remember, I don a stout leather jerkin on my way out to the yard. Odd apparel for a warm autumn evening but, as you see, necessary.

The menus for autumn travel through the breadth of temperatures that autumn brings. We start with the bright colours of tomatoes, ripened by the summer sun, cooked on crisp pastry, and finish with the soft browns and purples of mushrooms, chestnuts and quinces seemingly mirroring the darkening days and the need for warmth and comfort. At this time of year, classes revolve around the traditional farmhouse practices of preserving. Teaching people to cure and smoke a variety of food, make jams and chutneys, and break down pigs and ducks to make all manner of charcuterie is truly wonderful, and so readily adapted for the home environment. It's too easy to forget that not that long ago all this was actually a necessity. A long way from the true French autumn we chat about the peculiarities of the French farmhouse – the vast array of ceramic dishes used to keep confit, rillette and duck neck sausages safe from spoiling, the terrine tins and pate en croute moulds – and we giggle at our antipodean notions of the continent. Yet when I talk to my friends in France, who live on little plots like my own, their worlds are not so different to mine. Except, of course, they don't have to take wardrobe precautions to protect them from a flying grey cat.

With technology seemingly shrinking the distances between us, opportunities are emerging that would have been unthinkable twenty years ago. This menu pays homage to my friend Kate Hill, a woman I met through a cursory introduction over social media. The brother of one of my dearest friends suggested that Kate (an American living in Gascony) and I should get together for a cooking class when she visited Australia. And get together we did, resulting in a never-ending round of visits between rural Victoria and southwest France.

We talk and talk, among other things, about food production, cooking techniques, arts, science, ethics, the wonder of the pig and which are the most comfortable socks to wear in the kitchen. But most importantly, Kate is forever educating me about why French cooking is the way that it is – the importance of the village oven, the magic slow-braising that happens on a French stove, the beautiful nurturing of seasonal produce that is simple, easy and generations old.

This is a menu that brings early autumn produce to the fore: Kate's marvellous all-purpose pastry and her clafoutis recipe that has yet to fail are two of the standouts. The duck main course is a beautiful dish to make when you have no stock in the house, and the addition of prunes gives it a true Gascon flavour. This is a menu that suits lunch or dinner or that curious time on an autumn afternoon when the breeze blows softly, still laden with a little warmth from summer, but with the promise of crispness as the sun sets. And if you feel like making a new friend, find Kate at her marvellous Kitchen at Camont, online or in the flesh.

MENU ONE

EARLY AUTUMN	*Lunch or Dinner*

Fig wrapped *in* prosciutto

Gascon tomato *&* dijon tart

Duck legs braised *in* cider *with* prunes,
apple puree *&* potato boulangere

Raspberry clafoutis

Fig wrapped *in* prosciutto

SERVES 8

Some seasons figs are plentiful, others, they are scarce, but however they come you must make the most of them. One of the nicest ways to eat fresh figs is to wrap them in a thin slice of prosciutto. Simple and perfect, but you could also try first stuffing the figs with a strongly flavoured cheese, or a mixture of cheese and walnuts. I find that early in the season they are delicious raw, but once the cold nights have set in, the skin on the fig thickens up and they are much more delicious if you roast them.

8 figs, halved
80 g (2¼ oz) Roquefort or goat's cheese
4 walnuts, finely chopped (optional)
8 slices prosciutto, halved

If you are baking the figs, preheat the oven to 210°C (410°F).

Divide the cheese evenly among the figs. If you are using the chopped walnuts, mix them through the cheese before stuffing the figs. Wrap each fig half in a slice of prosciutto.

If the figs are soft, serve as they are. Otherwise, place on a baking tray and bake for 5 minutes. Serve warm.

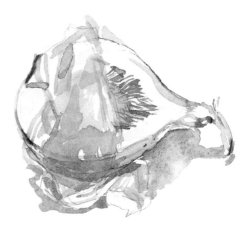

Gascon tomato & dijon tart

SERVES 8

I know that some people are a little timid about making their own pastry, but this recipe could change that. It is the most user-friendly pastry I've come across, and so forgiving that you can make it by hand on a benchtop or in a bowl, in a stand mixer with the paddle attachment, or in a food processor.

For this tart, I roll simple rectangles and fold the edges over to make a 'bande' tart. I love to use a variety of tomatoes of different colours and shapes to create a vibrant-looking tart, though if you have a lot of little tomatoes you tend to need more weight than if you are just slicing bigger varieties. For this reason I've given quite a broad range for the quantity of tomatoes – just use enough to give a generous layer over the pastry. The tart looks stunning on a long board or platter in the centre of the table and is delicious served with some simply dressed rocket (arugula) leaves.

1 quantity Kate's Excellent Shortcrust Pastry (see page 208)
60 g (2¼ oz) dijon mustard
500 g–1 kg (1 lb 2 oz–2 lb 3 oz) heirloom tomatoes of different shapes and colours, thinly sliced
100 g (3½ oz) goat's cheese (hard or soft, whichever you prefer)
salt flakes and freshly ground black pepper

Preheat the oven to 210°C (410°F). Line two 40 x 32 cm (16 x 13 in) baking trays with baking paper.

Divide the pastry in half and roll out into two 40 x 20 cm (16 x 8 in) rectangles. Lift carefully onto the trays and roll all the edges over to make a pretty border.

Lightly spread the mustard on each pastry rectangle, then cover with an overlapping pattern of tomatoes. Season with salt and pepper, then crumble or slice the goat's cheese sparingly over the top.

Bake on the top shelf of the oven for 20 minutes or until the pastry is golden brown. Remove, then slide carefully onto a wire rack to cool slightly.

Place on a platter to serve at the table or slice and plate individually. This is best cut with a sharp serrated knife.

Duck legs braised *in* cider *with* prunes, apple puree *&* potato boulangere

SERVES 8

I have structured this recipe so you cook the duck legs the day before, and heat them up in the oven with the potatoes shortly before serving. This will enable you to remove any excess fat from the cooking liquor, giving a more professional result.

Preheat the oven to 160°C (320°F).

Season the duck legs with salt and pepper. Heat the oil in a heavy-based saucepan over a medium heat and brown the duck legs well on all sides for 4–5 minutes. Transfer to a flameproof roasting tin in which the legs will fit snugly in a single layer.

Deglaze the saucepan with the apple cider and Calvados, then pour the liquid over the duck legs. Sprinkle over the thyme leaves and add the prunes.

Bring to the boil, then cover with foil and transfer to the oven. Braise for 1½ hours or until the duck legs are tender. Check occasionally to make sure the liquid has not evaporated too much – if it has, top up with a little water. Remove the duck legs and prunes from the sauce and place in a single layer in a container, then refrigerate overnight. Pour the cooking liquor into a separate container and refrigerate.

To make the potato boulangere, preheat the oven to 180°C (350°F) and butter a 22 cm (8½ in) gratin dish. Melt a knob of butter in a frying pan over a medium–low heat and cook the onion for 10–15 minutes or until soft and golden. Put a layer of potato on the base of the dish, then scatter over some onion and season. Repeat with the remaining potato and onion, finishing with a layer of potato. Pour in the stock and cover with foil, sealing around the edges.

8 duck legs
salt flakes and freshly ground black pepper
1 tablespoon olive oil
300 ml (10½ fl oz) apple cider
1 tablespoon Calvados
1 thyme sprig, leaves stripped
16 prunes
1 quantity Blanched Green Beans
  (see page 206)

POTATO BOULANGERE
unsalted butter, for cooking
1 onion, thinly sliced
800 g (1 lb 12 oz) yellow potatoes
  (such as nicola), thinly sliced
salt flakes and freshly ground black pepper
150 ml (5 fl oz) Chicken Stock (see page
  208), plus extra if needed

APPLE PUREE
20 g (¾ oz) unsalted butter
2 granny smith apples, peeled, cored and
  roughly chopped
salt flakes and freshly ground black pepper

About an hour before you are ready to serve, put the potatoes in the oven and bake for 45 minutes.

Meanwhile, take the duck legs, prunes and cooking liquor out of the refrigerator. Remove the layer of fat from the top of the sauce and discard. Place the duck legs, skin side up, prunes and sauce in a roasting tin.

After the potatoes have been cooking for 45 minutes, remove the foil and return to the top shelf of the oven for 15 minutes or until the top is golden. Add the duck to the oven to warm through.

To make the apple puree, melt the butter in a small heavy-based saucepan, add the apple and season with salt and pepper. Cook, covered, over a medium heat for 10 minutes or until soft. Puree with a hand-held blender or in a food processor. Taste and adjust the seasoning if necessary.

To serve, start with a pool of apple puree on each plate, add a little pile of beans and sit the duck leg up on the beans, then garnish with a couple of prunes and a little sauce. Serve the remainder of the beans in a bowl and place the gratin dish of potatoes in the centre of the table.

Raspberry clafoutis

SERVES 8

Clafoutis is really a fancy French name for a baked custard but, for such a simple dish, there are an awful lot of really, really bad clafoutis out there. This one is a gem, and many different types of fruit can be used at the bottom of it. I've used raspberries here, but they can be replaced with cherries, peaches or pears, or prunes soaked in Armagnac.

———————————

Preheat the oven to 180°C (350°F).

With a whisk, beat the eggs, sugar, flour and cornflour until thick and foamy. Gradually add the milk, thickened cream and Armagnac and whisk until well blended. This mixture can be made several hours ahead of time and refrigerated until you are ready to cook it.

Butter the sides and base of your chosen pan and dust with extra sugar. Place the raspberries evenly across the bottom of the pan, then carefully pour the batter over the raspberries. I like to put it in the oven after I have taken the main course out, which gives it plenty of time to bake while you are eating your duck.

Bake for 45 minutes or until puffy, golden and cooked in the centre (if you give it a little shake there should be no wobble). Remove and allow to cool slightly, then serve with cream.

4 eggs
60 g (2¼ oz) caster (superfine) sugar, plus extra for dusting
30 g (1 oz) plain (all-purpose) flour
30 g (1 oz) cornflour (cornstarch)
320 ml (11 fl oz) milk
320 ml (11 fl oz) thickened (whipping) cream
1 tablespoon Armagnac
250 g (9 oz) raspberries
pouring (single/light) cream, to serve

TIMELINE

THE DAY BEFORE

Cook the duck legs and refrigerate until ready to use.

THE DAY OF SERVING

Make the pastry and refrigerate.

Prepare the clafoutis mix and refrigerate.

Roll out the pastry into rectangles and roll the edges; refrigerate again.

1–2 HOURS BEFORE SERVING

Assemble the figs.

Assemble the tart, bake and set aside on a rack, ready to reheat later.

Top and tail the beans.

Butter and sugar the clafoutis dish.

Prepare the potatoes; plan to place in the oven about 30 minutes before you serve the tart.

Cook the apples, make the puree, and place in a small saucepan with a lid, ready to be reheated.

TO SERVE

Serve the figs; if roasting, turn up the oven for a few minutes, roast the figs and then return to 180°C (350°F).

Reheat the tart for 10 minutes while the potatoes are cooking.

Remove the tart from the oven, uncover the potatoes and place the duck in the oven to reheat.

Serve the tart.

Cook the beans, gently reheat the apple puree, then serve the main course.

But just before you sit down, place the raspberries in the clafoutis dish, pour over the custard and transfer to the oven – don't forget to set a timer, then go and enjoy your duck.

Remove the clafoutis and let it rest for 5–10 minutes before serving.

Luxe. That's the only word to describe this menu. Highly worked, high skill levels, fiddly to the extreme but full of ingredients that cry out to be revered above all others. Smoking at home takes a little practice, but this duck fillet is deceptively easy and is a wonderful way to start exploring the curious world of smoked food.

The main course features veal. Veal used to be easily accessible, with most dairy farmers raising their 'bobby' calves on the farm. With the rise of the multinationals and a fall in the international milk price, it is no longer viable to follow the old ways, so many farmers have no choice but to ship their calves off uncomfortably early. Yet some persist and unlikely alliances are formed. I get to use veal twice a year, in spring and autumn. A friend who farms dorper lamb works with a biodynamic milk farmer in her area. She buys the calves and he raises them to 12 weeks old, lovingly fed on biodynamic milk, and then she takes over and sells the veal from her farmers' market stall. If you want to cook veal, always seek out ethically farmed meat. Go to your local farmers' markets and ask questions – you may find the stories you hear are even more delicious than the meat.

Back to the menu though: the veal is paired with shallots, chestnuts and mushrooms. The shallots and chestnuts take patience, but, as the veal is special, it is only fitting that the accompaniments follow suit.

To finish, we master the art of puff pastry and marvel at the perfection of a ripe pear. For me, the Doyenne du Comice is a pear of such beauty and flavour that it is worth all the work in this dish. A true labour of love.

MENU TWO

EARLY – MID AUTUMN	Lunch or Dinner

Smoked duck fillet salad
with apple *&* radicchio

Paupillette *of* veal *with* chestnuts,
shallots *&* mushrooms

Pears *in* puff *with*
salted caramel sauce

Smoked duck fillet salad *with* apple & radicchio

SERVES 8

I love the process of smoking food. If you are new to it, though, there are a few basics to get your head around before you start.

For all its rudimentary simplicity, smoking is quite a scientific process. Smoke is made up of over two hundred components that help preserve food – some parts retard the oxidation of fat, others inhibit the growth of microbes which can cause food to go off. The process is broken into two main categories: hot smoking and cold smoking. Hot smoking cooks the fish, meat or vegetables, whereas cold smoking only imparts a smoked flavour, so the product can be cooked later or eaten raw. The food needs to be dry before it can be smoked, often overnight in the refrigerator (uncovered); this is where the food develops a slightly tacky skin, the 'pellicle', which helps the smoke flavour penetrate. But if you dry it for too long, the smoke will have trouble penetrating.

This recipe is a really great way to start your interest in smoking at home. Good-quality smoking chips and sawdust are readily available at barbecue shops these days. For smoking in a wok you need a fine chip or coarse sawdust – not the large sort of chips used for barbecues.

To make the cure, mix together all the ingredients and pour enough into a glass, ceramic or plastic container to cover the base. Place the duck fillets on the cure, skin side down, then cover with the rest of the cure. Refrigerate for 2 hours. Rinse the cure off the duck fillets and pat dry, then place on a clean plate and dry, uncovered, in the refrigerator for 8 hours.

Line a large wok with foil, place the smoking chips on the bottom and position a rack in the wok. I like to render the duck, skin side down, a little before smoking, so heat a frying pan over a medium heat, add the breasts, skin side down, and cook until golden.

4 duck breasts, trimmed of excess fat
2 tablespoons smoking chips or sawdust

CURE
150 g (5½ oz) salt flakes
150 g (5½ oz) soft brown sugar
2 bay leaves
2 teaspoons black peppercorns

APPLE & RADICCHIO SALAD
1 head radicchio
100 g (3½ oz) rocket (arugula) leaves
2 large cooking apples
1 tablespoon clarified butter
100 g (3½ oz) walnuts
salt flakes and freshly ground black pepper
10 chives, snipped

SIMPLE DRESSING
25 ml (¾ fl oz) apple cider vinegar
25 ml (¾ fl oz) white wine vinegar
50 ml (1¼ fl oz) extra-virgin olive oil
100 ml (3½ fl oz) grapeseed oil
salt flakes and freshly ground black pepper

Turn them over and seal the other side. Place the wok over a high heat, position the breasts on the rack and cover with a lid. When the smoke starts, turn the heat down to medium–low and smoke for about 15 minutes. The duck fillets need to be pink in the middle. Remove and rest for at least 10 minutes before use – the breasts can be eaten hot or cold.

To make the salad, preheat the oven to 180°C (350°F). Break up the head of radicchio, then wash to remove any dirt and pat dry. Do the same with the rocket. Peel and quarter the apples, then cut each quarter in half again to give 8 pieces for each apple. Melt the clarified butter in a frying pan over a medium heat. When hot, carefully add the apple and cook on one side until golden brown, then turn over and cook the other side to an even golden-brown colour. Remove and drain on paper towel.

Place the walnuts on a baking tray and toast in the oven for 10 minutes. Remove and sprinkle with a little pinch of salt flakes, then set aside to cool.

To make the dressing, whisk together all the ingredients and season to taste.

To assemble the salad, cut the duck fillet into very thin slices. Toss with the salad leaves, warm apple pieces, walnuts and chives, and gently toss through the dressing. Season with a little salt and pepper. The salad can be plated individually or on a large platter to share at the table.

Paupiette *of* veal *with* chestnuts, shallots *&* mushrooms

SERVES 8

A paupiette is a thin slice of meat wrapped around a minced meat mixture and fastened with a thin bacon rasher and string. The parcels are then baked in white wine and stock with various flavourings. Paupiettes are found all over France, in many different guises – in fact, they are so ubiquitous that most French people simply buy them already assembled from their butcher. Paupiette de veau is synonymous with Normandy cuisine, where so much dairy farming occurs and there is a plentiful supply of veal. Here, I'm serving it with some stars of autumn: chestnuts, shallots and mushrooms. I think these are delicious with Mashed Potato (see page 206) and a bowl of green vegetables – sprouting broccoli is particularly lovely in autumn.

This dish features two ingredients that I use a lot in my cooking. My preferred cut of bacon is known as kaiserfleisch, which is bacon made from the belly with no eye. You might also know it as streaky bacon. The other is quatre epices, a French spice mix made with cloves, nutmeg, ginger and pepper, which is used in both sweet and savoury dishes. You can make a little pot yourself, or buy a commercial blend.

1.5 kg (3 lb 5 oz) veal schnitzel
1.25 kg (2 lb 12 oz) minced (ground) veal
large pinch of salt flakes
¼ teaspoon quatre epices
¼ teaspoon freshly ground black pepper
2 tablespoons chopped flat-leaf
    (Italian) parsley
16 slices kaiserfleisch (streaky bacon)
24 French shallots
olive oil, for drizzling
unsalted butter, for cooking
16 chestnuts
250 g (8 oz) button mushrooms
vegetable or grapeseed oil,
    for cooking
125 ml (4 fl oz) white wine
250 ml (9½ fl oz) Veal or Chicken Stock
    (see page 208)

Start by assembling the paupiettes. Examine your pieces of schnitzel: you will need to trim them down to 16 somewhat even-sized pieces. Hand-mince any trimmings with a kitchen knife and add to your minced veal. Place each piece of veal between two pieces of plastic wrap or baking paper and beat gently with a meat mallet to an even thickness.

Place the minced veal in a bowl and season with salt, quatre epices, pepper and 1 tablespoon of the parsley.

Mix well to combine. Lay out all your pieces of veal on a clean surface and divide the mince stuffing evenly among them – it will be about 80 g (2¾ oz) for each. Roll up to make 16 neat parcels and wrap each one in a slice of kaiserfleisch. They should hold together nicely, but if you are unsure you can fasten with kitchen string as well.

I like to prepare each of the vegetables separately and add them to the paupiettes when they are cooked. Start with the shallots.

Preheat the oven to 180°C (350°F).

The easiest way to peel a lot of shallots at once is to blanch them. Bring a saucepan of water to the boil, add the shallots and bring back to the boil, then strain. Rinse under cold water. Peel the shallots, and place in a baking dish. Season with salt and pepper, sprinkle with olive oil and a knob of butter. Roast for about 20 minutes until golden brown, then remove and set aside.

Meanwhile, cut a cross in the bottom of each chestnut and place in a shallow baking dish. Roast for 10–15 minutes or until the chestnuts are bursting out of their shells. Remove from the oven and prepare yourself: the next step is the tedious bit. While they are still very hot, carefully peel the chestnuts. This is best done by picking them up in a cloth, removing the hard outer casing and, with the tip of a small knife, removing the skin around the flesh. If they cool and become too hard to peel, pop them back in the oven for a minute or two. Continue until they are all peeled (don't worry if they break up into little pieces).

Continued ...

Paupiette continued ...

Wipe away any dirt from your mushrooms and trim the stalks. If the mushrooms are tiny, leave them whole; cut larger mushrooms into halves or quarters. Heat 2 tablespoons of vegetable or grapeseed oil and a knob of butter in a frying pan over a high heat and cook the mushrooms for 10 minutes or until golden brown. Season, then remove from the pan and set aside.

Now, all of the above steps can be done well in advance and refrigerated until needed.

When you are ready to cook the paupiettes, preheat the oven to 180°C (350°F).

Heat a little vegetable or grapeseed oil a frying pan over a medium heat and cook the paupiettes on both sides until golden brown. (You will probably need to do this in batches.) Transfer to a gratin dish or baking dish that will hold them snugly in a single layer.

Deglaze the frying pan with white wine, add the stock and bring to the boil. Pour over the paupiettes. Ideally, the liquid should come about halfway up the side of the parcels. Bake for about 30 minutes, then remove from the oven and scatter the mushrooms, shallots and chestnuts over the paupiettes. Return to the oven and cook for a further 10 minutes. Remove from the oven and carefully remove the string, if used. Scatter with the remaining parsley and serve, preferably at the table in the baking dish.

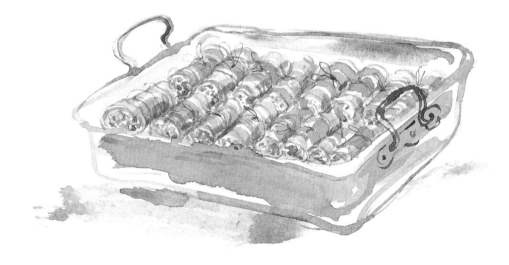

Pears *in* puff *with* salted caramel sauce

SERVES 8

Now, before I barrel into this recipe, let's talk about pears and puff pastry. It is perfectly acceptable in this day and age to buy good-quality puff pastry. Just make sure that you get all-butter puff – the one made with 'pastry margarine' is just not very nice. Homemade puff pastry takes some practice to get right; however, it is a very beautiful thing when you do. Put it on the list of things to try when you have oodles of spare time. Kitten likes making puff. He did a very funny photo shoot once where he was wrapped in the dough, just like Beatrix Potter's Tom Kitten.

Pears are one of my favourite fruits – their shape, their flavour, their texture. All just delicious. I'm lucky enough to grow a number of varieties of pears, although the Doyenne du Comice is definitely the star. When choosing pears for this tart they need to be ripe, but not too ripe. I find it also works best to choose a nice compact pear.

———————————————

To make the poached pears, combine the sugar, 1 litre (35 fl oz) of water and vanilla bean in a large saucepan and bring to the boil. Reduce to a simmer, then add the pears and gently poach until just cooked. The time will vary, depending on the ripeness and variety of the pears, but start checking with a skewer after about 7 minutes. When cooked, remove the pan from the heat. The pears can be stored in the syrup until you are ready to use them.

To make the salted caramel sauce, combine the sugar and 60 ml (2 fl oz) of water in a large heavy-based saucepan and stir over a low heat until the sugar has mostly dissolved. Increase the heat to high and bring to the boil. Use a brush dipped in water to wash down any sugar crystals from the side of the pan, but do not stir the syrup.

As soon as the syrup starts to turn an amber colour, remove from the heat and swirl it around the saucepan. The caramel will continue to cook and become darker after it has been removed from the heat, but if it does not become a rich amber colour, put the pan back on the heat for 5 seconds, then remove and swirl to mix.

1 quantity Puff Pastry (see page 209)
whipped pouring (single/light) cream,
  to serve

POACHED PEARS
1 kg (2 lb 3 oz) granulated sugar
1 vanilla bean, split lengthways
  and seeds scraped
4 'perfect' pears, peeled

SALTED CARAMEL SAUCE
225 g (8 oz) granulated sugar
125 ml (4 fl oz) pouring (single/light) cream
60 g (2¼ oz) unsalted butter, cut into cubes
1½–2 teaspoons salt flakes or fleur de sel

Off the heat, immediately add the cream, whisking constantly. The caramel will rapidly bubble up, but keep whisking until it has stopped bubbling. Add the butter and salt and whisk until the butter has completely melted and is mixed into the caramel. Leave to cool before using, or immediately pour the hot caramel into clean heatproof jars and store in the refrigerator. It will keep for up to a month – it will thicken when chilled, so reheat before using.

Preheat the oven to 210°C (410°F) and line a large baking tray with baking paper.

When you are ready to assemble the tarts, roll out the pastry to a thickness of about 4 mm (3/16 in). Make yourself a homemade pear-shaped stencil out of stout cardboard – it should be about 1.5 cm (1/2 in) bigger than the pears. Cut eight pear shapes from your pastry and chill while you prepare the pears.

Carefully remove the pears from the syrup with a slotted spoon and drain on paper towel.

Cut them in half lengthways and remove the cores. Place the pastry cutouts on the prepared tray and top each one with a pear half, cut side down.

Bake for 15 minutes or until the pastry is risen and golden brown. Reduce the temperature to 170°C (340°F) and bake for another 10 minutes to cook the pastry through. Remove from the oven.

Serve each tart with a generous helping of caramel sauce and some whipped cream.

TIMELINE

THE DAY BEFORE

Cure the duck fillets, then rinse, pat dry
and refrigerate.

Assemble the paupiettes and refrigerate.

Make the puff pastry.

Poach the pears and refrigerate.

THE DAY OF SERVING

Prepare the salad ingredients and refrigerate.

Make the dressing.

Prepare the vegetables for the paupiettes.

Roll out the puff pastry.

Assemble the tarts and refrigerate.

Make the caramel sauce.

1 – 2 HOURS BEFORE SERVING

Smoke the duck fillets and set aside at
room temperature.

Make the mashed potato and set aside
somewhere warm.

Place the paupiettes in the oven.

TO SERVE

Pan-fry the apple pieces and assemble
the duck salad.

Serve the duck salad.

Gentry reheat the mash on the stovetop, finish the
paupiettes and cook the broccoli.

Increase the oven temperature to 210°C (410°F).

Serve the main course.

When you have finished eating the main, cook the
tarts, then serve hot with the sauce.

There's something about that time of year when the cold starts creeping in. Suddenly there is kindling to split, wood to be stacked and fires to be lit. The pattern of the day changes inexorably. There are no more long afternoons when there is always enough daylight – the darkness descends quickly and, until I adjust, there's a slight panic to make sure that all the farmhouse chores are done: the poultry put away, the vegetables picked for tomorrow and the fires prepared so there are no unnecessary trips out into the darkness. While many an autumn day can start with a cruel frost, the weather is often glorious as the day wears on. And when I'm feeling organised, there is no better time to invite people to lunch.

This is a menu that I love for an autumn lunch. The pate and the components of the cake can be made several days ahead, leaving you time to focus on the partridge on the morning of your lunch. Partridges are curious little birds – bigger than a quail and smaller than a spatchcock, with a light gamey flavour and texture that is both surprising and delicious. I long to raise them here, alongside all my other poultry. One day.

MENU THREE

MID — LATE AUTUMN	*Lunch or Dinner*

Pate en croute

Partridge *with* coq au vin sauce
& roasted parsnips

Concorde cake

Pate en croute

SERVES 8

The marvellous thing about serving charcuterie of any sort is the relaxed nature of the dish. Good French farmhouse platters just beg to sit on a table and be talked over. Conversation reigns as you and your guests, without even realising it, consume large amounts of terrine or pate with bread and accompaniments. There's no real mystery to a pate en croute – it's really just a good terrine mix set in pastry instead of being wrapped in caul fat or kaiserfleisch or the like. If you don't feel like going to the bother of making pastry and aspic, you can certainly make this recipe as a terrine. Just line a terrine mould with thinly sliced bacon, fill with the terrine filling, cover and bake in a water bath at 160°C (320°F) for about 1¼ hours or until the internal temperature is 65°C (150°F). I serve the pate en croute with dijon mustard, salad greens, cornichons and any other delightful pickled thing you might have in your store cupboard.

_____

To make the aspic, place all the ingredients, except the salt and pepper, in a large saucepan along with 2 litres (70 fl oz) of cold water. Bring to the boil, then reduce the heat and simmer for 2 hours, regularly skimming any foam off the surface. Strain, return to the cleaned saucepan and reduce for another 10 minutes. Adjust the seasoning if necessary, then set aside to cool completely.

Preheat the oven to 180°C (350°F).

To make the terrine filling, heat a frying pan over a medium heat and saute the spinach until wilted. Remove and set aside to cool in a bowl. Add the remaining ingredients to the cooled spinach and mix well.

Roll out the pastry to a thickness of about 2 mm (1/16 in). Line your pate en croute mould or standard terrine tin with the pastry, leaving a little hanging over the side to attach the lid to. Cut a piece of pastry the same size as the top of the mould for the lid.

1 quantity Kate's Excellent Shortcrust Pastry (see page 208)
1 egg, whisked with a little water

ASPIC
1 pig's trotter (you may need to order this in advance from your butcher)
1 bay leaf
1 carrot, roughly chopped
1 onion, roughly chopped
6 peppercorns
salt flakes and freshly ground black pepper

TERRINE FILLING
200 g (7 oz) English spinach
300 g (10½ oz) pork shoulder, minced
225 g (8 oz) boneless skinless chicken thigh, minced
150 g (5½ oz) veal, minced
225 g (8 oz) pork fat, minced
2 scant tablespoons salt flakes
½ teaspoon freshly ground black pepper
½ teaspoon quatre epices
1 garlic clove, finely chopped
2 tablespoons chopped flat-leaf (Italian) parsley
3 sage leaves, chopped
3 thyme sprigs, leaves stripped and chopped
40 ml (1¼ fl oz) Armagnac
1 egg

Spoon the terrine filling into the pastry case, pressing down firmly and smoothing the surface. Attach the pastry lid, pressing gently to seal, then cut a hole in the middle and decorate with pastry scraps, if you like. Brush with the egg wash.

Bake for 1–1¼ hours or until a cooking thermometer inserted in the centre reads 65°C (150°F). Set aside to cool completely.

Melt the aspic over a low heat, then set aside to cool completely. Pour the cooled aspic into the pastry case through the hole at the top, then allow to set in the refrigerator overnight. Cut into slices to serve.

Partridge *with* coq au vin sauce *&* roasted parsnips

SERVES 8

Game birds in Australia are not quite what you'll find in Britain or Europe. They are never quite as 'gamey' as the real thing, but there are a number of farmers who still grow game birds for our market. I love to do this dish with the coq au vin–style sauce, as it adds a little more oomph to our delicate little partridges. You will often come across partridges in fine poulterers in autumn; if not, ask your butcher if they can be ordered in.

I like to serve these birds with a gratin dish of Creamed Potatoes (see page 207) and a bowl of Blanched Green Beans (see page 206).

———————————————

Preheat the oven to 180°C (350°F).

Bring a saucepan of water to the boil, add the shallots and bring back to the boil, then strain. Rinse under cold water. Peel the shallots, and place in a baking dish. Season with salt and pepper, sprinkle with olive oil and a knob of butter and roast for 20 minutes or until golden brown, then remove and set aside.

Heat 40 g (1½ oz) butter in a frying pan over a medium heat and cook the mushrooms until golden brown. Set aside.

Increase the oven temperature to 220°C (430°F).

Inspect your partridges. If they have come with their heads you will need to chop them off. Remove the first two joints of the wing, and check the cavity for any internal organs. Wipe the cavity and dry the outside with paper towel.

16 French shallots
salt flakes and freshly ground black pepper
olive oil, for cooking
unsalted butter, for cooking
200 g (7 oz) small mushrooms
8 partridges
6 thyme sprigs, leaves stripped
12 juniper berries
8 thin slices kaiserfleisch (streaky bacon)
4 parsnips, cut into large wedges
2 tablespoons Cognac
125 ml (4 fl oz) red wine
100 ml (3½ fl oz) Reduced Veal Stock
   (see page 208)

Put the thyme leaves, juniper berries, 100 g (3½ oz) butter and a pinch of salt and pepper in a mortar and mash together with the pestle. Spread this butter all over the birds, particularly on their breasts, then wrap a slice of kaiserfleisch around each bird. Place in a flameproof roasting tin, breast side up, and arrange the parsnip wedges around the birds. Roast for 30 minutes. If the kaiserfleisch looks like it's in danger of becoming too crisp, peel it off the birds and set it aside.

Remove the birds and parsnips from the roasting tin and set aside to rest, covered loosely with foil to retain the heat. Put the roasting tin over a medium heat, pour in the Cognac and mix with the pan juices, then add the red wine and stir to dissolve all the bits stuck to the bottom of the tin. Bring to the boil and boil until the sauce has reduced by half. Add the shallots, mushrooms and reduced veal stock and continue to boil for another 5 minutes or until the sauce has reduced to a velvety consistency.

Carve the birds off the breastbone, arrange on plates with the roasted parsnips and spoon over the sauce.

Concorde cake

SERVES 8

This cake always make me giggle. It was created by French pastry chef Gaston Lenotre in 1969 to celebrate the first flights of the Concorde aeroplane. I giggle because this blousy chocolate confection always reminds me of an over-the-top bathing cap and seems to have nothing in common with the beautiful sleek lines of the plane it was named after. That said, it has a certain 'je ne sais quoi' and is a good choice for entertaining as the components can be made the day before and assembled on the day you wish to serve it.

———————————————

Preheat the oven to 150°C (300°F) and line a large baking tray with baking paper.

To make the meringue, sift together the cocoa powder and icing sugar. In a stand mixer, whip the egg whites to stiff peaks, then add 1 tablespoon caster sugar and beat in. Add the remaining caster sugar in batches, then gently fold in the cocoa mixture.

Scoop the meringue into a piping bag fitted with a 1 cm (½ in) plain nozzle and pipe three 18 cm (7 in) rounds onto the prepared tray. Pipe the rest in strips (the length doesn't matter as you will be breaking them up later). Place in the oven and bake for 1 hour. Turn off the oven and allow the meringues to cool in the oven with the door propped open.

To make the chocolate mousse, melt the chocolate and butter in a heatproof bowl set over a saucepan of barely simmering water. Stir until smooth and well combined, then whisk in the egg yolks. Whip the egg whites to soft peaks, then beat in the caster sugar. Gently fold the whites into the chocolate mixture, then cover and refrigerate until needed.

To assemble, spread a thin layer of mousse (about a quarter of it) on each meringue disc and place on top of each other. Seal the outer edge with the remaining mousse. Decorate the top and side with the broken strips of meringue. Sift over icing sugar and cocoa powder if you wish to decorate further. Serve with the whipped cream.

Dutch (unsweetened) cocoa powder and pure icing (confectioners') sugar, to decorate (optional)
whipped pouring (single/light) cream, to serve

MERINGUE

50 g (1¾ oz) Dutch (unsweetened) cocoa powder
160 g (5¾ oz) pure icing (confectioners') sugar
9 egg whites
220 g (7¾ oz) caster (superfine) sugar

CHOCOLATE MOUSSE

240 g (8½ oz) dark (55%) chocolate, broken into pieces
150 g (5½ oz) unsalted butter
4 egg yolks
6 egg whites
2 tablespoons caster (superfine) sugar

TIMELINE

THE DAY BEFORE

Make the shortcrust pastry.

Cool the stock for the aspic.

Make the pate en croute filling.

Assemble and bake the pate en croute.

Make the veal stock.

Prepare the partridge.

Make the meringue.

Make the chocolate mousse.

ON THE DAY

Fill the pate en croute with aspic.

Strain and reduce the veal stock.

Prepare the parsnips.

Assemble the Concorde cake and refrigerate.

Whip the cream.

1 – 2 HOURS BEFORE SERVING

Assemble the creamed potatoes.

Arrange the partridge and parsnips in a baking tray.

Bake the potatoes – these can be reheated later.

Remove the potatoes and increase the oven temperature to 220°C (430°F).

TO SERVE

Place the partridge in the oven and set the timer.

Serve the pate en croute.

Return to the kitchen on the command of your timer.

Remove the partridge from the oven, make the sauce, cook the beans and reheat the potatoes in the oven.

Carve the birds and serve.

Enjoy the birds.

Serve the Concorde cake with whipped cream.

Deep, deep into autumn, there is no escaping the cold. A warm breeze is an ever-fading memory and the sun, when seen, is flanked by cold air and cloaked in timidity. Kitten is ensconced in front of the fire box, nesting quietly in his felt pods; Fenn is hunting mice and rats as they become easier prey, being drawn to the warmth of the poultry houses; and Tommy prefers to be snuggled in his sheepskin than brave the frosty chill of the early mornings for a walk. The last of the summer crops are harvested, and the shed and verandah are filled with beans drying in their pods and quinces quietly waiting their turn to be cooked.

So, as the nights become longer and colder, here is a beautiful menu to warm your body and heart.

MENU FOUR

LATE AUTUMN	*Lunch or Dinner*

Stuffed quail wrapped *in* prosciutto
with baked figs

Navarin *of* lamb

Roasted quince *with* spiced quince cake
& whipped ricotta

Stuffed quail wrapped *in* prosciutto *with* baked figs

SERVES 8

There is something really delicious about cooking meat in milk. The Italians love to use this technique with pork but here I wrap boned and stuffed quail in prosciutto and cook them in the oven in a nice warm milk bath. The quail are served simply on a bed of rocket with a luscious roasted fig alongside.

————————————

Preheat the oven to 200°C (400°F).

Bone the quail, leaving the first wing bone and drumstick bones in. (If you're not comfortable doing this, ask your butcher to do it for you.)

Put the ciabatta cubes, Roquefort and sage in a bowl and mush it up with your hands to combine.

Lay all the birds on the bench, skin side down, and divide the stuffing evenly among them. Re-form the birds and then wrap each one in a slice of prosciutto. Place in a baking dish that is large enough to hold the birds snugly in a single layer, then pour enough milk into the dish to come halfway up the side of the birds.

Place in the oven and roast for 10–15 minutes or until the birds are cooked – check by squeezing the leg meat to see if it's cooked through. The meat should push away easily from the bone. The tips should have a nice crispness and colour from the prosciutto. Once you've put the quail in the oven, cut the figs in half and place on a baking tray. Drizzle with a little olive oil and roast for about 7 minutes.

For each plate, lift the quail from the dish and place on a bed of greens. Prop half a roasted fig on each side, season to taste and serve.

8 jumbo quail

4 slices stale ciabatta, cut into 5 mm (¼ in) cubes

100 g (3½ oz) Roquefort or other strong blue cheese, crumbled

2 sage leaves, chopped

8 slices prosciutto

about 500 ml (17 fl oz) milk

8 figs

olive oil, for drizzling

100 g (3½ oz) rocket (arugula) leaves or other sharp salad greens

salt flakes and freshly ground black pepper

Navarin *of* lamb

SERVES 8

I love this traditional French country dish. I've cooked it with neck, shoulder or forequarter chops and they are all delicious. In late autumn I have baby carrots in the ground, the first of the new turnips and a stockpile of small potatoes from the garden. And I always make sure I save a stash of peas in the freezer, just for dishes like this, and also to remind me that while the oncoming winter may seem endless, spring is not really that far away.

Often when I am working alone in the kitchen I turn to the internet to reassure myself about classic recipes. It is one of the joys of the modern world that we have access to so many people's knowledge and heritage at the press of a button. As this is a dish that hails from Normandy, it seems only sensible to consult one of the best Norman chefs I know. This is a slightly reworked version of a recipe by the marvellous chef Philippe Mouchel, once from Normandy, now a proud Melburnian.

While this is great as a one-pot dish served simply with bread, you can always accompany it with Mashed Potato (see page 206) or a dish of Creamed Potatoes (see page 207).

———————————————

Heat the oil and a large knob of butter in a heavy-based saucepan over a medium–high heat. Add the lamb and cook until browned all over – you might need to do this in batches so you don't overcrowd the pan. Transfer the lamb to a plate.

Add the onion, carrot and a little more butter to the pan and cook, stirring, over a medium heat for 5 minutes or until softened. Drain off any excess fat, then add the flour and stir over the heat for 1 minute. Return the lamb to the pan, then pour in the wine and simmer until slightly reduced. Add the tomato, turnip, herbs and garlic, and enough stock to come three-quarters of the way up the lamb.

100 ml (3½ fl oz) grapeseed or olive oil

150 g (5½ oz) unsalted butter

2 kg (4 lb 6 oz) boned lamb neck or shoulder, cut into 5 cm (2 in) cubes

200 g (7 oz) onions, diced

200 g (7 oz) carrots, diced

1 tablespoon plain (all-purpose) flour

250 ml (8½ fl oz) dry white wine

4 tomatoes, diced

1 turnip, peeled and diced

1 rosemary sprig

1 thyme sprig

1 bay leaf

4 garlic cloves, roughly chopped

750 ml (25½ fl oz) Veal or Chicken Stock (see page 208)

salt flakes and freshly ground black pepper

250 g (9 oz) French shallots, trimmed and peeled

1 teaspoon granulated sugar

1 kg (2 lb 3 oz) new, small nicola or kipfler (fingerling) potatoes

300 g (10½ oz) baby carrots, peeled

300 g (10½ oz) baby turnips, peeled

80 g (2¾ oz) peas

crusty bread, to serve

Season well, then cover with a lid and simmer for 1 hour.

Meanwhile, heat the remaining butter in a small saucepan over a medium heat, add the shallots, sugar and some salt and cook, stirring, until lightly browned. Add a little stock or water and bring to the boil, then reduce the heat to low and cook for 10–15 minutes or until soft.

Put the potatoes in a large saucepan, cover with cold water and bring to the boil. Simmer for 5 minutes, then drain.

Remove the lamb from the pan, then strain the sauce through a fine sieve. Let the sauce settle so you can carefully skim the fat from the top. Return the sauce, lamb and potatoes to the pan and simmer, covered, for another 15 minutes.

Add the baby carrots and turnips and simmer for 10–15 minutes or until tender. Add the peas for the last 5 minutes.

Serve with good crusty bread to mop up the sauce.

Roasted quince *with* spiced quince cake *&* whipped ricotta

SERVES 8

While this is a brilliant combination of flavours and textures as a dessert, all three elements in this recipe can be enjoyed in splendid isolation or for other purposes. The cake is an excellent tea cake and keeps very well in a traditional cake tin. It is not too sweet and the quatre epices gives it a lovely savoury pepperiness – excellent for afternoon tea. The roasted quinces can be eaten as stewed fruit, used in frangipane tarts or just about any recipe calling for cooked quinces. And the whipped ricotta is a lovely accompaniment to most cakes and pastries, especially a good olive oil cake.

Preheat the oven to 120°C (250°F).

To make the roasted quince, put the sugar, 1 litre (34 fl oz) of water and spices in a large saucepan and bring to the boil, stirring to dissolve the sugar. Place the quince halves, cut side up, in a baking dish large enough to fit them snugly in a single layer. Pour the sugar syrup over the top. If you don't have enough syrup to cover the quinces, make a little more using equal quantities of sugar and water. Cover with a sheet of baking paper and then seal the baking dish with foil. Roast for at least 6 hours or until the quinces are dark purple and tender.

If you're not using them immediately, the quinces can be kept in their cooking syrup in the refrigerator for a couple of weeks. Before you use them, remove the core with a teaspoon.

To make the spiced quince cake, preheat the oven to 180°C (350°F) and line the base of a 20–22 cm (8–8¾ in) square cake tin with baking paper.

Sift the flour, spices and baking powder into a large bowl and add the salt. Put the golden syrup, quince syrup and butter in a small saucepan and warm over a low heat. Add the diced quince and

ROASTED QUINCE

1 kg (2 lb 3 oz) granulated sugar

1 vanilla bean, split lengthways and seeds scraped

1 cinnamon stick

12 quinces, peeled and halved

SPICED QUINCE CAKE

250 g (9 oz) self-raising flour

2½ teaspoons quatre epices

1 level teaspoon baking powder

pinch of salt flakes

200 g (7 oz) golden syrup or maple syrup

2 tablespoons quince syrup (from roasting the quinces)

125 g (4½ oz) unsalted butter

100 g (3½ oz) diced roasted quince

125 g (4½ oz) dark brown sugar

2 large eggs

240 ml (8 fl oz) milk

sugar and let the mixture bubble gently for a minute, giving it the occasional stir to stop the fruit sticking to the bottom.

Break the eggs into a bowl, pour in the milk and beat gently to break up the egg and mix it into the milk. Remove the butter and sugar mixture from the heat and pour into the flour, stirring firmly with a large metal spoon. Mix in the milk and eggs. The mixture should be sloppy, with no traces of flour.

Scrape the batter into the prepared tin and bake for 35–40 minutes or until a skewer inserted in the centre comes out clean. Leave the cake to cool in the tin for a few minutes, then invert onto a sheet of baking paper laid on a wire rack. The cake may be served warm or kept in an airtight container and served at room temperature. It will keep well for up to 5 days.

To make the whipped ricotta, place all the ingredients in a bowl and whisk together until stiff and well combined. Taste before serving – you can vary the amount of sugar to suit your personal taste.

To assemble the dessert, I cut a long thin piece of cake, prop half a warmed quince up against it and then place a quenelle of the whipped ricotta on one end of the cake.

WHIPPED RICOTTA
250 g (9 oz) fresh ricotta
1 tablespoon golden caster (superfine) sugar,
*   or to taste*
2 tablespoons pouring (single/light) cream
finely grated zest of ½ lemon
finely grated zest of ½ orange

TIMELINE

THE DAY BEFORE

Bone, stuff and wrap the quail.

Roast the quince (this can be done overnight if your oven has a timer function to turn itself off), then refrigerate.

THE DAY OF SERVING

Prepare and cook the lamb and all the vegetables except the peas about 3 hours before serving, then set aside at room temperature.

Make the quince cake.

Whip the ricotta and refrigerate.

Remove the roasted quince from the refrigerator.

I — 2 HOURS BEFORE SERVING

Prepare the salad leaves and figs for the quail dish.

TO SERVE

Cook the quail.

Plate and serve the quail, but start reheating the lamb on a low heat before leaving the kitchen.

Add the peas and heat through.

Serve the navarin of lamb.

Plate and serve the quince dessert.

WINTER

WINTER

Winter brings many challenges to my little farm, but it also brings great rewards. Winter is the season to eat well, very well, and a chance to explore some of the most robust recipes in the French farmhouse repertoire. It's easy to wallow in the proverbial and literal mud, in the gloom, and in the cold of the dark grey winter, but I don't. I relish the coming of winter. It is, in a curious way, my favourite season, and this helps me deal with the tasks that need to be attended to in late autumn and early winter. There is the beautiful process of putting the garden to bed for the winter. There are the wood heaps to address – piles and piles of neatly cut and split wood to see my fires through the winter. There are the poultry houses to prepare. Dirt and straw, wheeled in, to build up the levels of the yard in case there is a lot of rain and the poultry need to stand above the water level. Working through these tasks builds up a hunger, a need for good, rich, wholesome food that nurtures and nourishes the body through the cold months.

Kitten tends to sit the winter out. He has two daily excursions: one to accompany me out to the poultry in the morning to let the birds out of their pens, and two, to supervise me putting the birds away safely in the evenings. He does not linger outside, but returns quickly to the hearth where he can roll about doing his very best impression of a fur seal. Fenn, however, has other missions. As food for the field mice becomes scarcer in the paddock, the mice move in to the hen houses. Fenn spends countless hours, strong and still as a statue, waiting to pounce and devour the mice.

Life at du Fermier is delicious in the winter. I find that people respond to food very differently in the colder months. There seems to be an almost primeval need to be warmed and comforted by food, which makes my job incredibly easy. As customers come through the door into my cosy restaurant, warmed by the log fire and rich with the smells of freshly baked bread and braised meat, it is easy to sit them down, bring them a drink and then a procession of dishes that satisfy them to the bottom of their hearts.

And if eating in the depths of winter is a pleasurable experience, it has nothing on the joy of cooking at this time of year. For those who love to cook, the winter means there are few other distractions and you can settle into the warmth of your kitchen and cook to your heart's content. And for those who find winter hard on their nerves and their patience, cooking can often be a way out of the gloom.

As the season runs its course, there is so much to revel in. Thick, blanketing fogs that have you curled by the fire with a mug of hot soup and a good book. Crisp white frosts that make the yard look like it has been cleaned and whitened overnight, no slushy dirty mud to ruin the picture, as it has all been frozen solid. The joy of watching the fruit trees exposed – first as they drop their final leaves and then as the yearly prune defines their shape with a skeletal beauty. And, if we are really lucky, snow. That soft, white magic, not terribly common in our part of the world, that turns the little hamlet of Trentham into a winter wonderland.

Cassoulet is one of the flagships of the cuisine of southwest France. It is a marvellous winter dish that encapsulates the wonderful processes of the kitchen and the delight of sharing beautiful food at the table. Within France, it is a simple dish to put together as it is possible to buy the confit, the ventrenche and good Toulouse sausages at the local butcher or charcuterer. But I do think that even if I lived in France I would still love to go through all the processes to create a wonderful cassoulet, relishing in the time-honoured techniques of salting meat, preserving in duck fat and making my own sausages. This menu is for anyone who loves time in the kitchen. Once the cassoulet and dessert have been assembled, it is a menu that is easy to serve and maximises your time at the table, immersed in the conversations that good food ensures.

MENU ONE

EARLY WINTER	*Lunch or Dinner*

Gougeres

Goat's cheese & walnut salad

Cassoulet

Chocolate marquise dacquoise sandwich

Gougeres

SERVES 8

A gougere is a delicious little cheese pastry. I use gruyere here, but you can certainly replace it with blue cheese, cheddar or emmental if you prefer. Choux pastry is not difficult to make and the cooked puffs also freeze very well, so you can make these ahead of time. You can also make a gougere quite large, then split the cooked puff in two and fill it with salad – a delicious entree for the colder months.

100 g (3½ oz) cold unsalted butter,
  cut into small cubes
good pinch of salt flakes
140 g (5 oz) plain (all-purpose) flour
4 eggs
100 g (3½ oz) grated gruyere

Preheat the oven to 210°C (410°F) and line a large baking tray with baking paper.

Combine the butter and salt with 250 ml (9 fl oz) of cold water in a saucepan over a medium heat and stir until the butter has melted. Bring to the boil, then add the flour and stir over a low heat until the pastry forms a ball and comes away from the side of the pan. Transfer the dough to the bowl of a stand mixer fitted with the paddle attachment and allow to cool for a few minutes. Add the eggs one by one, mixing thoroughly after each addition. Add the cheese and mix through. (If you don't have a stand mixer, just put the dough in a mixing bowl and beat in the eggs and cheese with a wooden spoon.)

Spoon or pipe the pastry onto the prepared baking tray in balls about the size of walnuts, leaving enough room between each one to allow it to at least double in size. Place on the top shelf of the oven and bake for 10 minutes. Reduce the temperature to 160°C (320°F) and bake for another 10 minutes. Remove and cool slightly on a wire rack, then serve in a bowl to share. These are delicious warm or at room temperature. You can cook them ahead of time and reheat them if you wish.

Goat's cheese & walnut salad

SERVES 8

The French love a complex salad – it's the perfect entree, particularly before a rich main course. This is a classic flavour combination that really can't be beaten. If possible, it's best to find a chabichou or slightly matured log, but chevre will also be fine.

————————————

Preheat the oven to 180°C (350°F). Place the walnuts on a baking tray and toast in the oven for 10 minutes. Remove and sprinkle with a pinch of salt flakes, then set aside to cool.

Increase the oven temperature to 200°C (400°F).

Tear the lettuces into bite-sized pieces and mix together in a medium bowl.

To make the vinaigrette, whisk the oils into the vinegar, then add the shallot and season with salt and pepper.

Cut the baguette on the diagonal into 32 thin slices. Place on a large baking tray and crisp in the oven for 10 minutes. Remove from the oven, then while still warm, brush both sides with olive oil and rub with the cut garlic clove.

Cut the goat's cheese into 32 slices, then cover each crouton with a slice of cheese, return to the baking tray and warm in the oven while you assemble the salad.

Toss the lettuce with the walnuts and dressing, then arrange on a platter or individual plates. Dot the warmed croutons about and sprinkle with the chopped parsley.

100 g (3½ oz) walnuts
salt flakes and freshly ground black pepper
1 butter or bibb lettuce
1 small head radicchio
1 small oakleaf lettuce
½ Baguette (see page 204)
80 ml (2½ fl oz) olive oil
1 garlic clove, halved
200 g (7 oz) sharp goat's cheese
1 tablespoon chopped flat-leaf
  (Italian) parsley

VINAIGRETTE
50 ml (1¼ fl oz) walnut oil
100 ml (3½ fl oz) extra-virgin olive oil
2 tablespoons red wine vinegar
1 tablespoon finely chopped French shallot
salt flakes and freshly ground black pepper

Cassoulet

SERVES 8

The bones of this cassoulet recipe come from my wonderful friend Kate Hill. She has made cassoulet one of her absolute specialties and has finely honed her techniques to create this beautiful version. This is the basic, bona fide, easy-to-prepare, authentic, traditional, real, regional version of cassoulet that Kate teaches, cooks and eats in her French kitchen. The emphasis is on carefully combining very good ingredients, slow cooking and hearty enjoyment. I have included recipes for duck confit, Toulouse sausage and ventreche (salt-cured pork belly) so that you can make it totally from scratch and enjoy the extraordinary sense of achievement that will be your reward at the end. I leave the final word to Kate: 'Cassoulet is as much a state of mind as a recipe, and it should feed your spirit as well as your belly.'

The ventreche needs to be prepared about a week ahead and the sausages and confit should be made several days before you wish to serve your cassoulet, so start this recipe well ahead. There are various elements that may need to be ordered in advance, so tell your butcher what you are planning to make and see what he recommends. You will notice that the sausages have very specific measurements. This stems from good charcuterie practices where the salt quantity is 2% of the weight of meat.

Five days before ...

To make the ventreche, rub the pork belly all over with the salt. Place in a glass, ceramic or plastic container, skin side down, and leave to cure in the refrigerator for 5 days. Rinse off the salt and pat dry, then press the meat side into a generous amount of pepper. The ventreche is best if it is left uncovered while it is curing to dry a little. Once it has cured and you have rinsed it and applied the pepper, the ventreche will keep for a couple of weeks in the refrigerator. Again, it likes to be uncovered and aired – I hang it by a piece of kitchen string from one of the racks in the fridge.

VENTRECHE

500 g (1 lb 2 oz) piece of pork belly, skin on
30 g (1 oz) salt flakes
freshly ground black pepper

TOULOUSE SAUSAGE

680 g (1½ lb 8 oz) pork shoulder, finely chopped
220 g (8 oz) hard back fat (order from your butcher), finely chopped
18 g (⅝ oz) salt flakes
9 g (¼ oz) granulated sugar
5 g (⅛ oz) freshly ground black pepper
2 metres (6 ft 5 in) sausage casings (available from your butcher)

CONFIT DUCK

8 duck legs
3 tablespoons salt flakes
8 thyme sprigs
2 bay leaves
2 garlic cloves, crushed
1 kg (2 lb 3 oz) rendered duck fat

To make the Toulouse sausage, mix the pork and fat with the seasonings, then cover and place in the refrigerator overnight. The next day, mince the pork mixture and fill the sausage casings, then twist the casings to make sausages about 5 cm (2 in) long. The sausages are best if they hang in the refrigerator for 1–2 days.

To make the confit duck, lay the duck legs in a glass or ceramic baking dish, flesh side up, and sprinkle with the salt, thyme sprigs, bay leaves and garlic. Cover with plastic film and leave to marinate in the fridge overnight.

The next day, preheat the oven to 140°C (275°F).

Rinse the duck and pat dry with a cloth or paper towel. Return to the cleaned baking dish, skin side up. Melt the duck fat in a saucepan over a low heat, then pour over the duck legs. Place in the oven and cook for about 2½ hours or until the duck legs are very tender. Remove from the oven and leave the legs to cool in their fat, then refrigerate.

On the day ...

To make the braised beans, place all the ingredients in a large saucepan with 2 litres (68 fl oz) of water. Bring the mixture to the boil, then reduce the heat to low and simmer gently for 1 hour, or until the beans are just barely tender. The beans are done when their skins become papery and begin to collapse, and the cooking liquid becomes milky.

While the beans are cooking, start preparing the duck legs and sausages.

Remove most of the softened congealed fat from the surface of the duck legs and trim off any excess skin, leaving just enough covering to protect the meat. Joint the thigh from the drumstick, giving two neat packages of confit meat per person.

Continued ...

BRAISED BEANS

1 kg (2 lb 3 oz) dried white beans (such as cannellini or great northern beans), soaked overnight
1 onion, peeled
1 carrot, peeled
2 cloves
2 garlic cloves
500 g (1 lb 2 oz) ventreche
2 fresh pig trotters (order from your butcher)
100 g (3½ oz) fresh pork rind, rolled and tied with kitchen string
bouquet garni (with bay leaves, thyme sprigs, lovage and flat-leaf {Italian} parsley sprigs)
6 black peppercorns

Cassoulet continued ...

Heat a large frying pan over a medium–high heat and quickly brown the duck on both sides. Transfer to a plate, then brown the sausages. You want a nice hot pan to brown the skins, though you don't want to cook them all the way through at this stage as they will continue to cook in the cassoulet.

Preheat the oven to 240°C (475°F).

Time to assemble the cassoulet. Traditionally they are cooked in a deep, slanted dish called a cassole, which has a base that is half of the diameter of the top, but you can use a good-sized casserole or deep ovenproof dish.

Remove the bouquet garni, trotters, onion, carrot and pork rind from the beans. Chop the onion, carrot and rind into small bean-sized pieces and remove the tender meat from the trotters. Return to the beans and gently stir through. Using a slotted spoon, layer the cassole or dish with the beans, the confit and Toulouse sausage, then finish with a layer of beans. Adjust the seasoning of the bean broth – a little salt, perhaps some more black pepper. Now add this liquid to the dish until the beans are just covered. Save any remaining broth for basting if needed; otherwise, use it to make a bean soup later.

Put the cassoulet in the oven and cook for 30 minutes, then reduce the temperature to 175°C (340°F) and let the cassoulet bake slowly for 1½–2 hours. A wonderful crust forms during cooking so there is no need for a sprinkle of breadcrumbs (called for in some recipes) as the beans and starchy sauce do this by themselves.

Take your beautiful cassoulet to the table and set on a stout wooden board. Break the crust on top, ladle the steaming cassoulet into dishes and settle into an extraordinary experience.

Chocolate marquise dacquoise sandwich

SERVES 8

Watching my farmhouse menus take shape always makes me smile. In this one we start with a lovely light gougere, followed by a sharp, complex salad and then, wham – straight into a cassoulet! And to finish, one of the richest chocolate desserts I can muster. While it may seem odd to follow rich with rich, it works. This chocolate sandwich can be sliced thinly, and will last for many days in the fridge for a whole raft of tomorrows, but it's perfect paired with a glass of Armagnac, sitting by the fire, exploring all the conversations that were opened up over the cassoulet.

I like to make this in a thin, high terrine tin, but if you don't have one you can use a 24 cm (9½ in) springform tin and cut it into thin wedges.

———————————

To make the chocolate dacquoise, preheat the oven to 180°C (350°F) and line a large baking tray with baking paper. Using the tin you are going to use as a guide, draw three outlines on the paper. Turn the paper upside down so the pencil is away from the food but still visible through the paper.

Arrange the hazelnuts on another baking tray and toast for 15 minutes or until golden brown. Remove from the oven and set aside to cool.

Finely grind 70 g (2½ oz) of the hazelnuts with the icing sugar. Roughly chop the remaining hazelnuts and set aside for later.

Place the egg whites and a pinch of caster sugar in the bowl of a stand mixer fitted with the whisk attachment and beat on medium speed until stiff peaks form. Gradually add the remaining sugar, one-third at a time, incorporating each batch before adding the next. Continue mixing on medium speed for a further 5 minutes for a stronger, more developed meringue. Remove the bowl from the mixer and gently fold in the cocoa powder and hazelnut and sugar mixture until just combined.

pure icing (confectioners') sugar, for dusting
Dutch (unsweetened) cocoa powder, for dusting
whipped cream, to serve (optional)

CHOCOLATE DACQUOISE

80 g (2¼ oz) skinned hazelnuts
65 g (2¼ oz) pure icing (confectioners') sugar, plus extra for dusting
100 g (3½ oz) egg whites (about 3)
25 g (1 oz) caster (superfine) sugar
25 g (1 oz) Dutch (unsweetened) cocoa powder

CHOCOLATE MARQUISE

170 g (6 oz) dark (55%) chocolate, broken into pieces
120 g (4¼ oz) unsalted butter
2 eggs, separated
2 egg yolks
110 g (4 oz) pure icing (confectioners') sugar
3 tablespoons Dutch (unsweetened) cocoa powder
1 teaspoon caster (superfine) sugar
75 ml (2½ fl oz) pouring (single/light) cream

Transfer the dacquoise mixture to a piping bag fitted with a 1 cm (½ in) plain nozzle. Pipe the meringue around the outside of each outline on the prepared tray first, and then move inward to fill the disc. Sprinkle with chopped hazelnuts and dust twice with extra icing sugar. This will create a better crust on the surface.

Place the tray in the oven and bake for 15 minutes or until golden. Your dacquoise must be crisp on the outside, and soft and moist on the inside. Remove from the oven and set aside to cool completely. When cool, gently remove the meringues from the baking paper.

To make the chocolate marquise, melt the chocolate and butter in a heatproof bowl set over a saucepan of barely simmering water. Stir until smooth and well combined. Lightly beat the four egg yolks, then stir into the chocolate mixture. Sift together the icing sugar and cocoa powder and stir into the mixture.

Beat the egg whites to soft peaks, then add the caster sugar and gently fold into the chocolate mixture. Whip the cream to soft peaks and fold into the mixture.

To assemble, line your chosen tin with foil and then plastic wrap, leaving some overhanging the edges to help lift it out later. Trim the meringue layers to fit.

Place one meringue, face down, in the tin, then pour over half the marquise mixture. Add a second meringue, followed by the remaining marquise mixture. Top with the final meringue. Cover and chill overnight.

When you're ready to serve, invert the chocolate sandwich onto a serving platter and neaten the edges with a hot knife (heat the blade under hot water and wipe dry). Dust with icing sugar and then cocoa powder. You could also do a little decorative piping along the top with some whipped cream, if you like.

Cut into thin slices and serve.

TIMELINE

THE WEEK BEFORE

Pop into your butcher to buy your piece of pork belly and order your other meat needs to give them plenty of time.

Salt the pork belly and refrigerate.

2 DAYS BEFORE

Salt the duck legs and refrigerate.

Make the sausages and refrigerate.

THE DAY BEFORE

Make the dacquoise.

Make the marquise.

Assemble the dessert and refrigerate.

Cook the confit and refrigerate.

Soak the beans.

THE DAY OF SERVING

Cook the beans.

Oven toast the breadstick for the croutes.

Toast the walnuts.

Cook the gougeres.

Seal off the sausages and confit, assemble the cassoulet when the beans are cooked and place in the oven.

1 – 2 HOURS BEFORE SERVING

Prepare the salad greens, slice the cheese, top the croutes and have on a tray ready to go in the oven.

Unmould the dessert and decorate with whipped cream if desired; refrigerate.

TO SERVE

While your cassoulet is cooking you can do various things in the oven even if the temperatures are not exact.

Warm the gougeres and serve.

Warm the croutes and assemble the salad.

Take the VERY SPLENDID cassoulet to the table.

Slice the dessert at the table.

After the last menu I feel like I need a bit of a rest. There are occasions for massive traditional feasts like the cassoulet menu and then there are times when you need to cook and eat comforting, familiar dishes. This one meets the brief, and also answers a few common queries, like how to properly roast a duck.

The farm settles and quietens down in the winter. Something strange happens to Kitten's weight and he turns into a fat seal, seemingly overnight. He drifts from the fire to the bed, his lounging routine only abandoned to sprint outside with me, whatever the weather, to help let out or lock up the poultry. Often there is too much rain to do much outside and I must rely on the crops sown in late summer and early autumn for vegetables for the table. But then the magic happens. When it's cold and grey and wet, and my little town disappears under a fog, winter brings her own special black magic: the truffle. Like many places in the new world, we farm truffles in central Victoria. I have a run of holly leaf oaks that I hope will one day produce my own, but in the meantime I rely on my friend Georgie to go out with her dogs and sniff out some truffles for me. That gnarly black fungus puts a smile on most people's faces, except, of course, those who don't like mushrooms.

MENU TWO

EARLY — MID WINTER	*Lunch or Dinner*

Double-baked truffle
& gruyere souffle

Roast duck, brussels sprouts
& parsnips

Paris Brest

Double-baked truffle & gruyere souffle

SERVES 8

It might sound impressive but this really could not be easier to make. A double-baked souffle is simply a souffle made in a mould, turned out into a heatproof dish, covered in cream and rebaked. The addition of grated truffle makes it a little more spectacular, but if you don't have any truffle don't despair – there's nothing shabby about a simple double-baked gruyere souffle.

Preheat the oven to 180°C (350°F).

Melt 20 g (¾ oz) of the butter and grease eight 150 ml (5 fl oz) souffle dishes with it.

Melt the remaining butter in a small heavy-based saucepan. Add the flour and cook over a medium heat, stirring, for 2 minutes. Gradually add the milk, stirring constantly to smooth out any lumps. Bring to the boil, then reduce the heat and simmer for 5 minutes.

Stir in the gruyere, parmesan and grated truffle until smooth and well combined, then set aside to cool for a few minutes. Fold in three egg yolks (save the remaining yolk for another recipe) and season to taste.

Beat the egg whites to soft peaks, then fold quickly and lightly into the cheese mixture. Divide the batter evenly among the prepared dishes and smooth the surface. Stand the dishes in a sturdy baking dish lined with a tea towel and pour in boiling water to come two-thirds of the way up the side of the dishes. Bake for about 20 minutes or until firm to the touch and well puffed.

80 g (2¾ oz) unsalted butter
60 g (2¼ oz) plain (all-purpose) flour
350 ml (12 fl oz) warm milk
75 g (2¾ oz) gruyere, grated
1 tablespoon freshly grated parmesan
2 tablespoons grated truffle
  (about 20 g/¾ oz), plus extra truffle
  to garnish
4 eggs, separated
salt flakes and freshly ground black pepper
500 ml (17 fl oz) pouring
  (single/light) cream

Remove the souffles from the oven – they will deflate and look
wrinkled, but this is fine (we all have days like that). Allow to rest for
1–2 minutes, then gently ease them out of the dishes and invert onto
a large plate covered with plastic film. Leave until needed.

To serve, place the souffles upside-down in individual buttered
ovenproof gratin dishes (or you could put them in one big dish, as
long as they are not touching). Pour over the cream to moisten them
thoroughly, then return to the oven for 15 minutes. The souffles will
look swollen and golden. Shave a little extra truffle over each one
and serve immediately.

Roast duck, brussels sprouts & parsnips

SERVES 8

Roast duck seems to be the dish that I hear the most stories about. They're often funny, but always feature the dreaded tough duck. Having heard many dinner party horror stories and people regaling me with how lovely their duck was only to say 'the duck I had at such and such a restaurant was horrid', I now understand why roasting a whole duck seems to be an experience that vexes an inordinate number of people.

I feel that the confusion comes from the fact that we are familiar with lovely rare roasted duck breasts and slow braised or confited duck legs. It's the mystery of how to get the whole bird delicious that flummoxes people.

Perhaps think of it like this. A good-sized duck takes a couple of hours to roast. A quarter of the way into that two hours, the breasts are cooked beautifully pink but the legs are tough and still partly raw. Half way into the cooking process the breasts are starting to become seemingly overcooked, but the legs are still tough. Three-quarters of the way and the skin is starting to look delicious, the legs are starting to soften up but the breast meat looks dry. This is when most people have a bit of a panic and take it out, thinking it looks nice, and end up serving a tough, dry bird. But, if you have patience and faith, that last half an hour of cooking time is where the magic happens. The skin is crisp and golden, the legs are tender and delicious and the breast meat is rich, succulent and soft.

Preheat the oven to 220°C (430°F).

Scatter the vegetables over the base of a flameproof roasting tin large enough to accommodate all four ducks comfortably.

At this point you can prepare the ducks in one of two ways: either place them on the vegetables whole, or cut them in half, removing the backbone, and lay them on the vegetables, skin side up. Scatter over the thyme sprigs and season well with salt and pepper.

Add a little water to the roasting tin so that the fat doesn't burn while the ducks are cooking.

3 carrots, cut into small cubes
3 onions, cut into small cubes
3 celery stalks, cut into small cubes
4 small ducks
8 thyme sprigs
salt flakes and freshly ground black pepper
125 ml (4 fl oz) port
60 ml (2 fl oz) Reduced Veal Stock
  (see page 208)
1 quantity Blanched Brussels Sprouts
  (see page 206)

PARSNIP PUREE

1 kg (2 lb 3 oz) parsnips, peeled and
  roughly chopped, coarse core removed
500 ml (17 fl oz) milk
1 bay leaf
salt flakes and freshly ground black pepper

ROASTED PARSNIPS

1 kg (2 lb 3 oz) parsnips, peeled and
  cut into wedges
olive oil, to coat
salt flakes and freshly ground black pepper

Roast for 1 hour, basting every 15 minutes or so.

To make the parsnip puree, combine the parsnip, milk and bay leaf in a saucepan and bring to a simmer. Cook gently over a low heat for 45 minutes or until the parsnip is very soft. Remove the bay leaf and puree the parsnip in a blender with some of the milk. You are looking for a spreadable consistency so don't add all the milk if it is going to make it too thin. Season to taste with salt and pepper. You can make this ahead of time and reheat it later on the stovetop.

After an hour, turn the oven down to 160°C (320°F) and roast the ducks until tender (when you push at the leg meat it should be soft and yielding) – this will take the best part of another hour. Start checking after about 40 minutes.

To make the roasted parsnips, toss the parsnip wedges in enough olive oil to coat, then place on a baking tray and put in the oven about 15 minutes before the duck comes out. When you remove the duck, place the parsnips on the top shelf and turn the oven up to 200°C (400°F). They should crisp up in 5–10 minutes. Remove from the oven and season with salt and pepper.

Remove the duck from the oven. If you have roasted the ducks whole, you can now carve the meat off the frame. If you have cooked them in halves, turn them over and remove all the bones from the underside.

Strain the fat off the vegetables, leaving the vegetables in the tin, then place the tin over a medium heat. Deglaze with the port, stirring to lift off any bits stuck to the base of the tin, then add the reduced veal stock and bring to the boil. Strain into a saucepan or jug.

To serve, make a pool of puree on each plate or a serving platter and place a mound of roasted parsnips to the side. Balance half of the duck on the parsnips, then decorate with the sprouts and spoon over the sauce.

Paris Brest

SERVES 8

Gorgeous Paris Brest is a show stopper and utterly delicious, but much easier to make than you might think. It was originally developed to commemorate the Paris–Brest–Paris cycling race, and is as good today as it was in 1910, when men used cake for stamina rather than silly energy drinks. I fill mine with pastry cream, praline and whipped cream.

Preheat the oven to 210°C (410°F). Line a baking tray with baking paper and draw a 22 cm (8½ in) circle on the paper with a pencil. Turn it upside down so the pencil is turned away from the food but still visible through the paper.

Spoon the choux pastry dough into a piping bag fitted with a 1 cm (½ in) plain nozzle, then pipe the dough around the circle a couple of times. If you have too much dough, use it up by making a few choux puffs. Scatter the almonds on top of the pastry. Place on the top shelf of the oven and bake for 10 minutes, then reduce the heat to 160°C (320°F) and cook for another 25 minutes. Remove and cool completely on a wire rack.

To make the pastry cream, place the milk and vanilla in a heavy-based saucepan and bring to scalding point. Remove from the heat. In a stand mixer fitted with the whisk attachment, whisk the sugar and egg yolks for 5 minutes or until pale. Add the cornflour paste, then the hot milk and whisk until combined. Return the mixture to a clean saucepan and place over a medium heat. Bring to the boil, stirring constantly, until the mixture is smooth and thick. Remove from the heat and place in a clean container. Closely cover the surface with plastic wrap to prevent a skin forming and store in the refrigerator until needed.

To make the praline, preheat the oven to 180°C (350°F). Spread out the flaked almonds on a baking tray and toast in the oven for 10 minutes or until golden brown.

1 quantity Choux Pastry (see page 209)
50 g (1¾ oz) flaked almonds
300 ml (10 fl oz) pouring (single/light) cream, whipped
pure icing (confectioners') sugar, for dusting

PASTRY CREAM
500 ml (17 fl oz) milk
½ vanilla bean, split lengthways and seeds scraped
125 g (4½ oz) caster (superfine) sugar
6 egg yolks
50 g (1¾ oz) cornflour (cornstarch) mixed with a little extra milk to form a paste

PRALINE
100 g (3½ oz) flaked almonds
200 g (7 oz) granulated sugar

Place the sugar in a heavy-based saucepan with just enough water to moisten it. Bring to the boil, stirring with a metal spoon until the sugar has dissolved, then cook without stirring until it becomes a nice golden colour.

Scatter the almonds over a greased baking tray with sides and evenly pour the toffee over. Allow to set, then pulverise in a food processor, leaving it a little chunky. If you are making this ahead of time, store it in an airtight container in the freezer until needed.

To assemble, split the choux ring in half horizontally. Place the bottom half on a serving platter, pipe in the pastry cream, scatter with the praline, then pipe on the whipped cream. Top with the top half of the choux ring, dust with icing sugar and serve. Don't assemble this too far in advance otherwise it will go soggy – do it 2 hours ahead at the most and pop it in the refrigerator.

TIMELINE

THE DAY BEFORE

Make the pastry cream.

Prepare the praline.

THE DAY OF SERVING

Make the choux pastry ring.

Make the souffles, remove from the moulds and refrigerate.

Prepare the ducks for roasting.

I—2 HOURS BEFORE SERVING

Place the ducks in the oven.

Cook the parsnip puree and set aside in a small saucepan, ready for reheating.

Whip the cream and place the cream and the pastry cream in separate piping bags fitted with large plain nozzles; refrigerate.

Place the parsnips in the oven to roast.

Here, we deviate from the individual recipes and behave a little like a professional cook: when the duck is ready, remove it and the parsnips from the oven; place the duck on a resting tray, reserving the roasting tin for making the sauce.

TO SERVE

Cook the souffles in cream and serve immediately.

Increase the oven temperature to 200°C (400°F).

After the souffles have been eaten, boil the water for the sprouts and return the parsnips to the oven.

Make the duck sauce.

Reheat the parsnip puree.

If you are worried that your duck has cooled too much, pop it back in the oven for a few minutes.

Assemble the plates of duck.

When the main course is finished, assemble the Paris Brest and serve at the table.

Food can be a funny thing. The seasons definitely dictate what we want to eat, through the way the weather makes us feel and the availability of produce. One of the strangest things that I have noticed during my years at du Fermier is that a lot of the menus take on a colour palate that is completely uncontrived, and we only become aware of it as we plate each course. The colours align with the seasons (and sometimes with my moods). This menu is always known as the white menu. And while it's not completely white all the way through, it has the muted tones of winter.

MENU THREE

MID — LATE WINTER	*Lunch or Dinner*

Celeriac *&* potato soup
with parsley puree *&* soft poached eggs

Chicken *in* mourning roasted crowns

Hazelnut puddings *with* malt ice cream

Celeriac & potato soup *with* parsley puree & soft poached eggs

SERVES 8

This rich white soup is comforting and creamy in its own right but, enriched with a poached egg and sharpened by a brilliant green puree, it starts moving into sublime territory.

_____

Melt the butter in a large heavy-based saucepan over a low heat, add the onion, leek and garlic and cook gently for 10–15 minutes or until they are very soft. Be careful not to let them colour. Increase the heat and add the potato, celeriac and most of the stock. Bring to the boil, then reduce the heat and simmer for 20 minutes or until the vegetables are tender. Allow to cool for a few minutes, then puree in a food processor – always puree the bulk of the vegetables first and then adjust the consistency with the remaining stock. Pour the pureed soup into a saucepan, add the cream and warm through. Taste and adjust the seasoning.

To make the parsley puree, bring a large saucepan of heavily salted water to the boil. When boiling rapidly, add the parsley and boil for 10 minutes. Drain, reserving some of the water, and immediately put the parsley in iced water to refresh it. Drain again, place in a blender with 1–2 tablespoons of the reserved cooking water and blend until very smooth. Add the olive oil and season to taste.

To serve, gently reheat the soup in a saucepan (if necessary). At the same time, heat another saucepan of water with salt and a dash of vinegar and bring to the boil. When the soup is nearly hot enough to serve, break all the eggs into a clean bowl, make a whirlpool in the boiling water and pour in the eggs. Bring back to a simmer and poach for 5 minutes or until soft. Gently lift out the poached eggs with a slotted spoon and drain on a tray or plate lined with paper towel.

Ladle the soup into bowls and top each one with a poached egg. Decorate with parsley puree and finish with a grinding of black pepper.

50 g (1¾ oz) unsalted butter
2 onions, thinly sliced
1 leek, white and pale green parts only, thinly sliced
2 garlic cloves, crushed
300 g (10 oz) white potatoes, diced
1 large celeriac, peeled and diced (you'll need about 600 g/1 lb 5 oz)
2 litres (70 fl oz) Chicken Stock (see page 208)
300 ml (10½ fl oz) pouring (single/light) cream
salt flakes and freshly ground black pepper
dash of white vinegar
8 bantam or very small eggs

PARSLEY PUREE
2 bunches flat-leaf (Italian) parsley, leaves picked and washed
1 tablespoon olive oil
salt flakes and freshly ground black pepper

Chicken *in* mourning roasted crowns

SERVES 8

This dish encapsulates what I love so much about French cooking. Firstly, roast chicken is my favourite thing – the unsalted butter, the crisp skin and the soft white breast meat. But it's the French sense of humour that often comes with naming dishes that I particularly love. 'Poulet demi deuil' literally translates as 'chicken in half-mourning', referring to the veil-like appearance of the black truffles tucked beneath the chicken skin. For me it ranks alongside 'truites en chemise' (whole trout with pastry or bayonne ham around their middles as if they were sporting a modesty panel) as a classic French dish with a wonderfully silly name.

Traditionally this dish is made with a whole chicken but I like to use only the crown (the two breasts still on the bone) so they can be roasted until silky and succulent. I also like to trim the first two joints from the wing. These have a tendency to singe a little in the oven, and I have an appreciative little dog at my feet when I cook this at home. Tommy loves a little treat of a chicken wing, as does Kitten, but he tends to 'play' with his chicken tidbits a bit too much.

Cauliflower is abundant during winter and goes beautifully with the roast chicken. A generous serve of creamed potatoes finishes the picture.

***

Preheat the oven to 200°C (400°F).

Remove the first two joints of the wing tips and feed them to your version of Tommy. Carefully insert your fingers between the skin and breasts of the chicken, moving all the way to the end of the breasts and gently peeling back the skin. Take your time with this as you don't want to tear it.

4 crowns cut from 1.6 kg (3½ lb) chickens (ask your butcher to do this for you)

1 black truffle (around 50 g/1¾ oz)

240 g (8½ oz) unsalted butter

1 garlic bulb, halved horizontally through the cloves

8 thyme sprigs

4 bay leaves

salt flakes

1 cauliflower, cut into florets

1 quantity Creamed Potatoes (see page 207), to serve

Finely shave two-thirds of the truffle. Place four or five large slices of truffle on each breast underneath the skin. Place a thin slice (about 30 g/1 oz) of butter on each breast. Pull the skin back over the breasts to secure the truffle slices and butter. Cut the garlic into four even pieces and place one inside each chicken crown, along with a couple of thyme sprigs and a bay leaf.

Place the four crowns in a spacious baking dish and season generously with salt. Roast for 45–50 minutes or until the juices run clear when pierced with a skewer in the thickest part of the meat. Once the chicken is cooked, remove to a resting plate and cover with foil to keep warm. Add the cauliflower florets to the pan and roast in the cooking juices for about 7 minutes.

I like to present this as a shared dish. Carve the chicken breasts off the bones and arrange them on a large platter. Scatter the warm cauliflower around the plate and drizzle with the cooking juices. Shave the remaining black truffle over the top and serve with creamed potatoes.

Hazelnut puddings *with* malt ice cream

SERVES 8

As it's truffle season, I have to include this dessert. The hazelnut pudding recipe comes from the very first months of my first proper job as an apprentice. That time is all a bit of a blur but I remember that I worked for some Austrians and I remember this recipe. In the eighties we served it with a kiwi fruit puree! Now, I serve it with a curious ice cream. Why curious? Well, I had a little excess of truffle that couldn't be wasted so I made a batch of ice cream with it. It was delicious but very familiar. It took me a while but eventually I worked out why it was so familiar: the truffle mixed with egg, cream and sugar suddenly tasted like malt. I never seem to have enough truffle to try the experiment again, but am delighted that it inspired this lovely malted ice cream that goes so perfectly with the puddings.

To make the ice cream, combine the milk and sugar in a saucepan and bring to scalding point, stirring occasionally. Meanwhile, place the egg yolks and a ladle of the milk mixture in a bowl and whisk together. When the milk reaches scalding point, pour in the yolk mixture, whisking constantly, then immediately remove from the heat and strain through a fine-mesh sieve.

Add the malted milk powder and stir to dissolve, then stir in the cream. Cool, then churn in an ice-cream machine according to the manufacturer's instructions.

To make the puddings, preheat the oven to 200°C (400°F). Grease eight dariole moulds.

Rub the skins from the hazelnuts, then blend in a food processor to form a paste.

MALT ICE CREAM
375 ml (12½ fl oz) milk
190 g (6½ oz) caster (superfine) sugar
6 egg yolks
50 g (1¾ oz) malted milk powder
375 ml (12½ fl oz) thickened
  (whipping) cream

HAZELNUT PUDDINGS
135 g (5 oz) toasted hazelnuts
100 g (3½ oz) unsalted butter
100 g (3½ oz) caster (superfine) sugar
125 ml (4 fl oz) rum
6 eggs, separated
35 g (1¼ oz) cornflour (cornstarch)

BURNT ORANGE CARAMEL SAUCE
250 g (9 oz) granulated sugar
juice of 6 oranges, strained

Place the butter and half the sugar in a stand mixer fitted with the paddle attachment and beat until pale and creamy. Add the rum, egg yolks, cornflour and hazelnut paste and mix until combined.

Whisk the egg whites to soft peaks, then add the remaining sugar and whisk again. Gently fold into the hazelnut mixture.

Divide the mixture evenly among the eight moulds. Place the moulds in a large roasting tin and pour in boiling water to come two-thirds of the way up the side of the moulds. Cover with greased foil and bake for 25 minutes. Remove the moulds from the tin.

To make the burnt orange caramel sauce, place the sugar in a heavy-based saucepan with just enough water to moisten it. Bring to the boil, stirring with a metal spoon until the sugar has dissolved, then cook without stirring until it becomes a dark golden colour. Carefully pour in the orange juice and whisk until smooth and well combined. Set aside to cool.

To serve, divide the caramel sauce among eight plates. Turn out the puddings onto the pool of sauce and serve with the malt ice cream.

TIMELINE

THE DAY BEFORE

Make and churn the malt ice cream.

THE DAY OF SERVING

Cook the soup.

Make the parsley puree.

Prepare the chicken crowns.

Make the orange caramel sauce.

1–2 HOURS BEFORE SERVING

Make the hazelnut pudding mixture,
but stop before you whisk and add the egg whites.

Prepare the creamed potatoes.

Place the chicken in the oven.

TO SERVE

Place the potatoes in the oven.

Reheat the soup, poach the eggs and assemble
the soup.

Remove the chicken from the oven. Place on a plate
and cover with foil to keep warm. Put the cauliflower
in the chicken roasting tray and roast.

Meanwhile, whisk the egg whites, finish the pudding
mixture and spoon into the moulds.

Carve the chicken.

Just before you serve the main course,
place the puddings in the oven (turn on a timer!).

Serve the chicken.

Remove the puddings from the oven when cooked
– they are quite happy to sit if you are not ready to
eat them.

Turn the puddings out and serve with the sauce and
ice cream.

There is little doubt that food is one of the most valued tools of celebration. Feasting is part of most of our lives, no matter what ethnic, religious or cultural backgrounds we come from. The winter solstice is a date that is perfect for exploring some of my own heritage and traditions. A time when I can sit with friends and immerse myself in food that represents a traditional Anglo Saxon Christmas. The menu revolves around dishes that seem reserved for this special celebration, notably glazed ham and plum pudding. I love special occasion food. It is so full of memories and history. It is also a menu that the guests at my restaurant love me to reprise each and every winter, when the fog is thick and there is a bit of snow on the ground.

MENU FOUR

| *Lunch or Dinner*

Cold smoked trout

Glazed Berkshire ham

Roasted pork loin *with*
crackling *&* vegetables

Plum pudding *with* Armagnac custard

Cold smoked trout

SERVES 8

Next to bacon, smoked fish is probably the most loved smoked food. I always start mine in a traditional gravlax-style cure, but in recent months I have developed a penchant for using fine bourbon after the smoke. It enhances the flavour and works very well if you want to serve a little apple salad with your smoked fish. These days I prefer to cure ocean trout rather than salmon, as I find the flesh has a better texture, but feel free to substitute salmon here if you prefer. The smoked fish is absolutely delicious served with brioche and scrambled eggs for breakfast. It can also be sliced and eaten with some green salad leaves and sour cream, or served on little pikelets or blini.

The trick is to produce smoke with little heat so that the fish doesn't cook. To achieve this I use one large foil baking tray, two smaller foil containers, a rack, ice and foil. You will also need an old wok or pan you don't use for cooking any more to heat up the smoking chips. It's a bit cumbersome but it works in a domestic environment.

_____

Two days before ...

Mix together the sugar and salt. Place a sheet of foil on the bench, cover with plastic wrap, then spread with half the salt cure. Place the fish on top and cover with the remaining cure, then wrap tightly in the foil and plastic wrap and place in the refrigerator under a weight. (I use a house brick wrapped in foil for my weight.) Turn after 12 hours, then weight for another 12 hours. Remove the fish and wash off the cure, then pat dry and refrigerate, uncovered, for another 12 hours or so to dry.

400 g (14 oz) raw (demarera) sugar
500 g (1 lb 2 oz) salt flakes
1 kg (2 lb 4 oz) side of ocean trout, trimmed, bones removed
ice cubes, 2 handfuls of smoking chips or sawdust and 2 tablespoons Russian caravan tea, for smoking
splash of bourbon

The day before ...

To assemble your smoker, fill one of the smaller foil containers with ice and rest a cake rack on top. Place at one end of the large foil tray. Sit the fish on the rack. Position the other small foil container at the other end of the baking tray. Take a handful of smoking chips and 1 tablespoon of tea and heat in your designated smoking wok or pan over a high heat until it starts to catch. Encourage a little burn and then place the chips and tea carefully in the empty foil container as far away from the fish as possible. Working quickly, cover the tray with foil to contain the smoke and smoke for 45–60 minutes. Discard the smoking chips and start again in the wok or pan with a new batch of ice chips and tea and smoke for another 45–60 minutes. There is no need to turn the fish.

The smoked fillet always loves to be rubbed with a little alcohol afterwards, in this case bourbon. It's worth doing as it removes a little of the acrid flavour from the smoke. For best results, wrap the fish and store in the refrigerator for 24 hours before you use it to give the flavours time to develop. Stored this way, the fish will last for a week at least. Slice and serve with your favourite accompaniment.

Glazed Berkshire ham

SERVES 8

I view buying a Christmas-style ham as a once-a-year investment.
A Berkshire or old-breed free-range ham will cost you up to $300
but it is absolutely worth it. The fat coverage is perfect for glazing
and baking, you can be assured of a well-bred and well-kept animal,
and the difference between a full ham on the bone and the boneless variety
is truly immense. Any ham not eaten will keep for at least two weeks, or
portions of meat can be cut off, wrapped carefully and frozen for later.
And, of course, the bones make the best pea and ham soup.

This beautiful ham is best served simply with lightly dressed sharp green
leaves and a bowl of boiled and buttered new potatoes, sprinkled with
chopped chives.

340 g (12 oz) orange marmalade
250 ml (8½ fl oz) orange juice
220 g (8 oz) brown sugar
1 tablespoon dijon mustard
5–6 kg (11–13 lb 3 oz) ham leg
cloves, for decorating

Preheat the oven to 200°C (400°F). Line a large baking dish with
baking paper, then place a lightly greased wire rack in the dish.

Place the marmalade, orange juice, brown sugar and mustard in a
saucepan over a high heat and whisk to combine. Bring to the boil,
then reduce the heat to low and cook for 3–5 minutes or until the
glaze has thickened slightly. Gently remove the skin from the ham
with your fingers, before using a knife to trim away any excess fat.

Use a small, sharp knife to score the ham in a diamond pattern, then
cover the hock with foil (to stop it from burning). Place the ham on
the rack in the baking dish. Gently press a clove into each diamond,
then brush the glaze all over the ham. Roast for 35–40 minutes or
until golden and caramelised, basting the ham with the glaze every
10 minutes or so.

Once the ham is glazed, it can happily sit for a couple of hours at
room temperature while you start preparing the main course. I like to
serve it at the table, making a great show of its beauty, and slicing it
abundantly.

Roasted pork loin *with* crackling *&* vegetables

SERVES 8

First we ate the leg, now it's time for the loin – roast pork loin and crackling is a magnificent presentation piece. As you will have gathered, this is an unashamedly traditional menu but be warned, there may be a lot of leftovers from all four courses. There is possibly already leftover smoked fish to eat with scrambled eggs, leftover ham to make croque monsieur with, there will almost certainly be some pudding for later on and, well, there might be some pork loin left too. My favourite thing to do in this situation is to freeze the leftover cooked loin, then shave it frozen (with a very sharp knife) and add it to udon noodles, cabbage and miso for a healthy one-pot dinner.

———————————————

Preheat the oven to 240°C (475°F).

I'm not very big on tying up pork loins neatly, but …

Season all the flesh you can get to with salt and pepper. Wipe the scored skin with a cloth doused heavily in white vinegar. Then, if you must, tie it in a neat roll.

Put the pork in a flameproof roasting tin. If you haven't tied it up, just lay it out flat, fat side up. Rub it with a little olive oil, then sprinkle the fat generously with salt and pepper and massage it in with your hands. Stuff the rosemary and garlic under and around the meat. Add 250 ml (8½ fl oz) of water to the roasting tin (this will help keep the fat from burning and smoking). Roast for 40–50 minutes. This burst of high heat will start the process of turning the fat into crispy crackling – try not to open the oven door so you don't let any heat out.

Reduce the oven temperature to 180°C (350°F). Place the vegetables around the pork loin, then return to the oven and roast for a further 50–60 minutes. The meat is pretty much self-basting but the vegetables will benefit from being turned and basted with the pan juices a couple of times. Remove from the oven and set the meat and vegetables to one side.

2 kg (4 lb 6 oz) piece of pork loin with belly
  and skin, scored by the butcher
salt flakes and freshly ground black pepper
white vinegar, for wiping
olive oil, for cooking
4–5 rosemary sprigs
3–4 garlic cloves
4 roasting (floury) potatoes, peeled and
  quartered
4 carrots, peeled and quartered
2 large turnips, peeled and quartered
16 French shallots or 8 baby onions, peeled
200 ml (7 fl oz) white wine
60 ml (2 fl oz) Reduced Veal Stock
  (see page 208)
1 savoy cabbage, shredded
50 g (1¾ oz) unsalted butter
1 tablespoon chopped flat-leaf
  (Italian) parsley

Place the roasting tin over a medium heat, tip in the wine and stir to remove any bits stuck to the bottom. Add the veal stock and bring to the boil, then strain into a jug.

Meanwhile, bring a large saucepan of water to the boil. Just before you are ready to serve, add the cabbage and cook for 3–5 minutes. I like it crunchy, but if you don't, cook it for a bit longer. Drain, then return to the pan with the butter and parsley and season to taste.

To serve, spread the cabbage on a large platter. Slice the meat and crackling and arrange on top of the cabbage (which will absorb all of its delicious juices). Arrange the vegetables around the outside and spoon over the sauce.

Plum pudding *with* Armagnac custard

SERVES 8 (WITH PLENTY OF LEFTOVERS)

I love eating plum pudding. Especially leftovers. If I'm feeling a little blue, tucked up in bed on a cold winter's night, surrounded by a snoring dog and sleeping cats, a bowl of plum pudding with some cold cream goes a very long way towards lifting my spirits. I tend to make pudding twice a year: once for classes I hold for Christmas cooking and for Christmas in the restaurant itself, and in the middle of winter for winter solstice celebrations. In my fridge at home, there is always a carefully wrapped but ever-diminishing piece of plum pudding, kept especially for little cheering treats.

I've made a number of puddings over the years but this one has become one of my favourites. It's a reworking of Nigella Lawson's fabulous ultimate Christmas pudding. As I did, feel free to alter the alcohol or fruit mix to your desired taste. Every Christmas baker must make the pudding their own.

I like to make one big pudding, in a 1.8 litre (61 fl oz) pudding bowl, but you can make individual ones or a series of different sizes. Just remember that smaller ones take less time to cook.

The night before ...

Put all the fruit in a bowl with the Armagnac and mix so the fruit is well coated. Cover with plastic wrap and leave to steep overnight or for up to a week.

When you're ready to finish the pudding mixture, bring a large saucepan of water to the boil – the pan needs to be big enough to hold your pudding bowl. Grease your bowl (or bowls) with unsalted butter.

Coarsely grate the cold suet or butter into a large mixing bowl, then add all the remaining ingredients (except the extra Armagnac) and mix together well. Add the steeped fruit and their liquid and combine thoroughly.

150 g (5½ oz) sultanas (golden raisins)
150 g (5½ oz) currants
150 g (5½ oz) roughly chopped prunes
175 ml (6 fl oz) Armagnac or Cognac
150 g (5½ oz) cold suet or unsalted butter
100 g (3½ oz) plain (all-purpose) flour
125 g (4½ oz) fresh breadcrumbs
150 g (5½ oz) dark brown sugar
1 teaspoon ground cinnamon
¼ teaspoon ground cloves
1 teaspoon baking powder
finely grated zest of 1 lemon
3 large eggs
1 medium cooking apple, peeled and grated
2 tablespoons golden syrup or maple syrup
125 ml (4 fl oz) Armagnac, extra (optional)

ARMAGNAC CUSTARD
500 ml (17 fl oz) milk
½ vanilla bean, split lengthways
    and seeds scraped
6 egg yolks
125 g (4½ oz) caster (superfine) sugar
50 ml (1 fl oz) Armagnac

Transfer the mixture to the prepared pudding bowl or bowls. Cover with two layers of baking paper and two layers of foil and secure with string, making sure the 'skirts' are tucked up so they don't draw in any water. Place in the pan of boiling water, making sure the water only comes halfway up the side. I like to place an egg ring at the bottom so the bowl is not directly on the heat. Boil for 5 hours, checking regularly that it hasn't boiled dry. Top up with more water if necessary.

Once cooked, the pudding will last in the fridge for months. During this time, I periodically splash a little Armagnac over it. However, the pudding is still delicious if you want to make it on the day. To reheat it, put a new paper and foil lid on it and boil for 3 hours.

To make the Armagnac custard, pour the milk into a saucepan, add the vanilla and bring to scalding point over a medium heat. Whisk the egg yolks and sugar for 5 minutes or until thick and pale. Pour the hot milk onto the yolk mixture and whisk to combine, then return to the saucepan and cook, stirring, over a medium heat for 7 minutes or until thickened. Remove from the heat and strain if required. Stir in the Armagnac, then pour into a heatproof jug.

When the pudding is ready, carefully take the bowl out of the pan, remove the foil and paper and invert onto a serving platter. Drizzle with the extra Armagnac if you want to set this beauty on fire, then serve with the Armagnac custard.

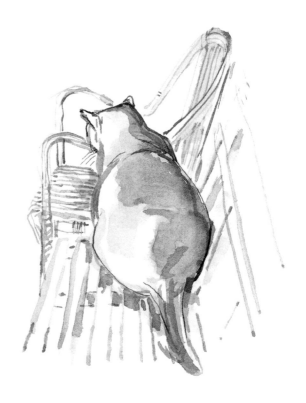

TIMELINE

2 DAYS BEFORE

Salt the fish.

Soak the fruit for the pudding.

THE DAY BEFORE

Smoke the fish and refrigerate.

Score the pork loin and tie (if required).

Make the pudding.

THE DAY OF SERVING

Prepare the ham for glazing.

Make the glaze.

Cut the vegetables for the pork loin.

3 HOURS BEFORE SERVING

Glaze the ham and set aside at room temperature.

Boil the pudding.

Make the custard and set aside at room temperature.

1 – 2 HOURS BEFORE SERVING

Check the pudding water.

Slice the trout.

Begin to roast the pork loin.

Check the pudding water.

TO SERVE

Check the pudding water.

Prepare a platter of smoked trout and serve with your choice of accompaniments.

Place the vegetables in the tin with the pork loin.

Check the pudding water.

Take the ham to the table, slice generously and serve.

Remove the pork from the oven.

Make the sauce.

Slice the pork.

Cook the cabbage.

Check the pudding water.

Serve a generous platter of pork and vegetables.

Unmould the pudding, place on a platter and serve at the table with custard.

Relax – you've earned it.

SPRING

SPRING

Spring is like a zephyr through your soul. Whether you love or hate winter, the coming of spring brings an innocence that softens even the least romantic of hearts. It starts with tiny, subtle changes. The winter is always strangely silent of tiny bird song, and then as spring creeps in they start whistling and chirruping in the cold of the dawn, as if winter had never been and their worlds are an eternal summer. Quiet, in contrast with the little birds, is the grove of silver birches. Each morning, on the way down the path, my gaze is drawn to them. Something about them seems a little fatter. And then, as I glance across one morning, there it is: the softest, most translucent haze of the cleanest green has appeared. From then on there is no stopping them, and within days the tiny leaves have taken on form and substance.

Likewise, under the thick mat of straw, deep in the dark wet earth, the asparagus starts to stir. Pushing up those first white spears, tentatively poking their noses above the bedding, only to be burnt off at first by the frosts. Then with a resilience and perseverance I can only admire, more and more emerge from the straw bedding, until there are hundreds of little asparagus soldiers saluting the morning sun. The air can still be bitingly cold and the frost harsher and more destructive than at any time of year, but something has shifted and there is hope. Hope and the promise of the sun warming the back of my neck as I go about my chores.

There is a lot of romance in the poultry yard too. I am not ashamed to admit that I come under the human sub-category known as poultry fanciers. The poultry run is set up to house five separate enclosures of chickens and geese. In late winter, I lock up all the chickens with their appropriate rooster. My favourite are the tiny little Columbian wyandotte bantams – chubby, friendly little birds that I think every farmhouse should have. They are colloquially named Carlos and the Chala Cartel, a nod to another vague obsession of mine, yet a murderous bunch of fictional drug lords they are not. Then there are the French marans, and they are murderous. There are two maran roosters – proud, arrogant birds, who defend their women with an intense ferocity, almost in the style of the French foreign legion. Here they are, strangers to these shores, doing their best to keep their lines clean. A stout stick and a piece of fencing iron as a shield usually keeps me safe. The rest of the chickens are kept as layers. The gander, like the maran roosters, gets a little protective – honking and charging at me whenever I appear. It's a careful dance when I'm trying to collect eggs, whether it be for cooking or incubating. But by the end of spring, I know I can look forward to an absolute abundance of new life.

Spring also brings an explosion of green, in every shade possible. New herbs emerge to be joyfully paired with peas, artichokes, asparagus and broad beans. There is much preparing and planting to be done for the coming seasons, and what starts as a soft and gentle breeze of memory becomes the strident and busy reality of new life and the abundant seasons to come.

Unfortunately, there are some things about the beginning of spring that aren't that pleasant. For a start it's still quite cold, and the garden can be downright depressing, with the remnants of the winter crops and a lot of black wet dirt, which goes from just wet to frozen and back again because of the frosts. And then there is the daily egg-collecting challenge. My normally friendly geese become outright bullies in the springtime. I'm not too keen on increasing my goose population so I have to bravely make the charge and steal their eggs. My reward is a bowl of enormous eggs, and I find many lovely things to make with them, including omelettes, glorious sponges, batters for naughty toad in the hole, and pasta. Delicious, strong, golden pasta.

This is a menu for when it's still cold, but you can just sense a change in the air and that winter is slipping out to stage left.

MENU ONE

EARLY SPRING	*Lunch or Dinner*

Goose egg pappardelle *with*
smoked trout, dill & creme fraiche

Braised beef shin

Lime tart

Goose egg pappardelle *with* smoked trout, dill *&* creme fraiche

SERVES 8

Now, if you don't want to make your own pasta or smoke your own freshwater trout, that's fine. These days, there's plenty of good fresh pappardelle and beautiful packaged smoked trout available to buy. But just in case you do, here is a bevy of instructions.

_____

To make the pappardelle, mound the flour on a work surface – a granite counter or wooden board is ideal. Make a well in the centre of the flour and add the eggs and salt. Using a fork, beat the eggs and salt as if making scrambled eggs. As you beat the eggs, use the fork to slowly incorporate the flour, starting from the inside edge and working around the well (be careful not to break the walls of the well or the eggs will spill out). Keep going until a dough starts to form and clump.

Using your hands, collect and incorporate the remaining flour, kneading the dough until it is no longer taking in any more flour. (Alternatively, put the dry ingredients in a food processor. Whisk the eggs together, pour into the processor and pulse until a dough forms.) Knead on a lightly floured surface for about 10 minutes or until the dough is smooth. Form into a ball, cover with plastic wrap and leave to rest for at least 20 minutes.

Once the dough has rested, lightly flour your work surface and cut the dough ball into quarters. Work with one piece at a time – cover the remaining pieces with a clean tea towel until you are ready to roll them out. Push the dough piece into a flat rectangle with the palm of your hand and dust lightly with flour. Feed it through the widest roller setting of a pasta machine. Dust lightly with flour again and fold it into thirds, then run it through the widest setting again.

300 g (10½ oz) creme fraiche
finely grated zest of 1 lemon
2 tablespoons picked dill sprigs
salt flakes and freshly ground black pepper

FRESH PAPPARDELLE
500 g (1 lb 2 oz) unbleached plain
  (all-purpose) flour
350 g (12½ oz) eggs (your choice of goose,
  duck and/or chicken eggs), weighed in
  the shell
½ teaspoon salt flakes

HOT-SMOKED RAINBOW TROUT
120 g (4¼ oz) salt flakes
100 g (3½ oz) soft brown sugar
2 teaspoons fennel seeds
2 rainbow trout
1 handful of dill or fennel fronds
2 tablespoons apple sawdust

Continue to feed the dough through the rollers, setting the rollers closer together each time until you reach your desired thickness – for pappardelle, it needs to be rolled to the second-last thickness in most pasta machines.

Lay the sheet of dough flat on a table and cut into 1 cm (½ in) wide ribbons. Hang the ribbons over a broomstick balanced between two chairs. Repeat these steps with the remaining dough. If you find the pasta gets a little large and unwieldy as you are rolling it, cut it in half for easier handling.

Allow the pasta to dry for 15 minutes, by which time it will have a slightly leathery texture. At this point you can cook it, but if you want to store it, let it dry completely, then gently remove it from the broom handle and store it in containers until you're ready to use it.

To make the hot-smoked rainbow trout, combine the salt, sugar, fennel seeds and 1 litre (35 fl oz) of water in a saucepan and bring to the boil to dissolve the dry ingredients. Set aside to cool completely.

Wash the fish thoroughly, removing any traces of blood. Place in a glass, ceramic or plastic container, pour over the brine to cover and leave for an hour in the refrigerator. Remove the fish from the brine, rinse and pat dry, then return to the refrigerator for another 3 hours to dry. Stuff the fish with the dill or fennel fronds.

Line your smoking wok with foil, then add the sawdust. Place a lightly oiled rack in the wok, then put the fish on the rack, leaving plenty of space around them for the smoke to circulate. Cover with a tight-fitting lid or foil and place over a medium heat. When wisps of smoke appear, reduce the heat to low–medium and smoke for about 15 minutes.

Continued ...

Goose egg pappardelle continued ...

Check to see if the fish is cooked through (if you press at the top of the fish it will feel firm). Remove from the heat and rest in the wok for another 15 minutes to give the flavours time to soften and develop. The smoked fish can be served warm or chilled, but is best eaten within 48 hours.

Shortly before you are ready to serve, bring a large saucepan of salted water to the boil.

Peel the skin from the fish, then remove the flesh in little chunks, being sure to remove any tiny pin bones. Set aside.

Place a large frying pan over a medium heat, add the creme fraiche and lemon zest and bring to the boil. Add the trout and reduce to a simmer.

The pasta will only take about 3 minutes to cook so you need to have your wits about you. Have a strainer ready in the sink and a warm serving platter or bowls at hand.

Place the pasta in the boiling water, stir gently and cook for 3 minutes. Test a little to see if it is al dente, then strain.

While this is happening, turn up the heat under the creme fraiche mixture and boil until it thickens and has large bubbles forming.

Add the cooked pasta to the cream sauce, scatter over the dill and stir through gently. Season well with salt and pepper and serve immediately.

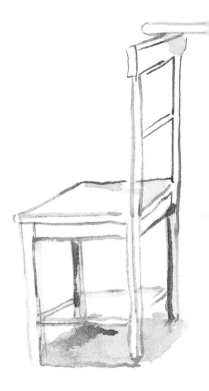

Braised beef shin

SERVES 8

I'm lucky enough to have a world-renowned wagyu beef farm
a few kilometres down the road. For some reason I thought that when
it came to stewing cuts, the fact that it was wagyu wouldn't make any
difference, but it certainly does. That said, if you can't get wagyu shin,
buy some shin meat that is from two-to three-year-old steers and you will
still get a lovely result. I like to cook the meat whole and pull it apart at
the table. Butchers often sell beef shin as gravy beef, so ask for a whole
piece of the muscle, with the bone out. I usually serve this with creamy
Mashed Potato (see page 206).

———————————————

Preheat the oven to 120°C (250°F).

Heat the oil in a large heavy-based frying pan over a medium heat.
Season the shin with salt and pepper, then sear in the pan until
brown on all sides. Transfer to a deep baking dish.

Add the onion, carrot, celery and garlic to the pan and cook over a
medium heat for about 10 minutes or until softened and beginning
to brown. Scatter the vegetables around the meat in the dish.

Discard any oil in the pan, then return it to the heat and deglaze with
the port, Cognac or Armagnac, stirring to dissolve all the bits stuck
to the bottom of the pan. Add the stock and bring to the boil, then
pour it over the meat in the dish. Cover with a sheet of baking paper
and then seal with foil. Transfer to the oven and cook for 8 hours.

By the end of the cooking time, the meat should be very dark and
soft. Carefully transfer the shin to a deep serving dish, then strain
the liquid into a saucepan, discarding the vegetables. Skim the fat
from the surface, bring to the boil and reduce to a rich, unctuous
consistency. This should take about 10 minutes, but it will depend
on how much evaporation has occurred during cooking. Pour the
sauce over the meat and scatter with the chopped parsley. Serve
with mashed potato.

60 ml (2 fl oz) olive oil
2 kg (4 lb 6 oz) whole beef shin, off the bone
salt flakes and freshly ground black pepper
2 onions, chopped
3 carrots, chopped
4 celery stalks, chopped
4 garlic cloves
150 ml (5½ fl oz) port, Cognac or Armagnac
1 litre (34 fl oz) Veal Stock (see page 208)
  or good-quality beef stock
chopped flat-leaf (Italian) parsley, to garnish
1 quantity Mashed Potato (see page 206)

Lime tart

SERVES 8

In early spring I am often the happy recipient of excess citrus fruit from local crops. If you happen to have access to an abundance of home-grown limes, this is a very lovely tart to make.

———————————————

Preheat the oven to 200°C (400°F) and grease a 28 cm (11 in) tart tin.

Take the pastry out of the refrigerator and roll it out on a well-floured surface to a 3 mm (⅛ in) thickness. Loop the pastry around your rolling pin, then gently unroll it over the prepared tin. Smooth down the pastry, removing any air bubbles trapped under the surface, then trim with scissors about 1 cm (½ in) above the edge and fold back and pinch together to form a neat edge.

Line the pastry with baking paper and fill with pie weights or uncooked rice or beans. (You can keep about 1 kg (2 lb 4 oz) rice or beans in your cupboard for this purpose and reuse them every time a recipe calls for blind-baking pastry.) Put the tin in the oven and blind-bake the pastry for 10–15 minutes or until the top edge starts to colour.

While the pastry is baking, make the filling. Whisk the eggs and sugar until well combined, then add the lime zest, lime juice and pouring cream, and stir thoroughly.

Remove the paper and weights from the pastry case and bake for a further 5–10 minutes or until golden all over. It is important that the pastry is fully cooked before you add the filling.

Reduce the oven temperature to 160°C (320°F).

1 quantity Sweet Shortcrust Pastry
  (see page 209)
5 eggs
250 g (9 oz) caster (superfine) sugar
finely grated zest of 3 limes
juice of 6 limes
200 ml (7 fl oz) pouring (single/light) cream
good-quality vanilla ice cream or thick
  (double/heavy) cream, to serve

Ladle the filling into the hot pastry case, then carefully return it to the oven and bake for 25–40 minutes. The exact cooking time depends on how effective your oven is. Don't forget that this is essentially a custard, which likes to cook nice and slowly. Bake until the tart is just cooked and the centre is slightly wobbly.

Allow to cool on the bench and serve at room temperature. You can refrigerate it overnight prior to serving, but I always prefer a tart whose pastry has not seen the refrigerator as it retains a delicious crispness. Serve with ice cream or thick cream.

TIMELINE

THE DAY BEFORE

Make the brine and chill.

Cook the beef shin, remembering it will take 8 hours, then remove from the sauce and refrigerate the two separately (this will set the fat in a hard layer on the sauce, making it easy to remove).

THE DAY OF SERVING

Brine the trout.

Make the pasta and refrigerate.

Roll and cut the pasta, then dry.

Roll the pastry and refrigerate.

Remove the trout from the brine and dry.

I—2 HOURS BEFORE SERVING

Smoke the trout.

Prepare the dill.

Blind-bake the tart shell.

Make the tart filling.

Bake the tart, set aside.

Make the mashed potato.

TO SERVE

Preheat the oven to 180°C (350°F), place the beef in a baking dish, add half the cooking liquor and heat in the oven.

Reduce the remaining cooking liquor over a low heat on the stovetop.

Cook the pasta and make the sauce.

Serve the pasta.

Warm the mashed potato.

Arrange the beef on a platter with the warmed mash and the reduced liquor poured over the meat.

Serve with green vegetables of your choice.

Serve the tart at the table with cream and/or ice cream.

In spring the three green vegetables that are always first off the rank in my garden are globe artichokes, peas and asparagus. This menu features all three. It is an alluringly simple menu designed to remind you of the beauty that comes from simple things.

The row of artichokes that I grow is a favourite haunt for Fenn, Kitten and Tommy. As the weather warms, it seems that the small field mice love to make their homes among these robust plants. Fenn, of course, hunts the mice out and catches them. Kitten watches on from the side, hoping Fenn will flush one out for him without him exerting any effort. And Tommy, fascinated by the rustling, trots up and down, often sticking his head into the plants with his bottom in the air and his straight little cairn terrier tail held aloft. Watching three happy animals enjoying the soft warmth of spring gives me so much pleasure as I busy myself harvesting its new-season bounty.

MENU TWO

EARLY — MID SPRING	*Lunch or Dinner*

Asparagus tart

Brined pork loin *with* peas,
artichokes *&* brown sage butter

Orange puddings

Asparagus tart

SERVES 8

This is the spring version of the tart I make in autumn with tomatoes. The fresh asparagus is paired with a bit of mustard, some salty feta, a lovely mixture of egg and a sprinkle of spring herbs to finish.

_____

Preheat the oven to 210°C (410°F). Line a 40 x 32 cm (16 x 13 in) baking tray with baking paper.

Divide the pastry in half and roll out into two 40 x 20 cm (16 x 8 in) rectangles. Lift carefully onto the tray and roll all the edges over to make a pretty border. Refrigerate while you prepare the asparagus.

Snap the ends off the asparagus so each spear is about 15 cm (6 in) long. Bring a large saucepan of water to the boil, add the asparagus and cook for 3 minutes. Remove and refresh in a bowl of iced water, then drain and pat dry.

Lightly spread the mustard on each pastry rectangle, then arrange the asparagus on top in lines. Season with salt and pepper, then crumble the feta sparingly over the top.

Bake on the top shelf of the oven for 20 minutes or until golden brown. Remove, then slide carefully onto a wire rack to cool slightly.

Grate the hard-boiled eggs in a line down the centre of the tart and sprinkle with the chopped herbs.

Place on a platter to serve at the table or slice and plate individually. This is best cut with a sharp serrated knife.

1 quantity Kate's Excellent Shortcrust Pastry (see page 208)
600 g (1 lb 5 oz) asparagus
70 g (2½ oz) dijon mustard
salt flakes and freshly ground black pepper
100 g (3½ oz) feta
4 hard-boiled eggs
1 teaspoon snipped chives
1 teaspoon chopped chervil
1 teaspoon chopped flat-leaf (Italian) parsley

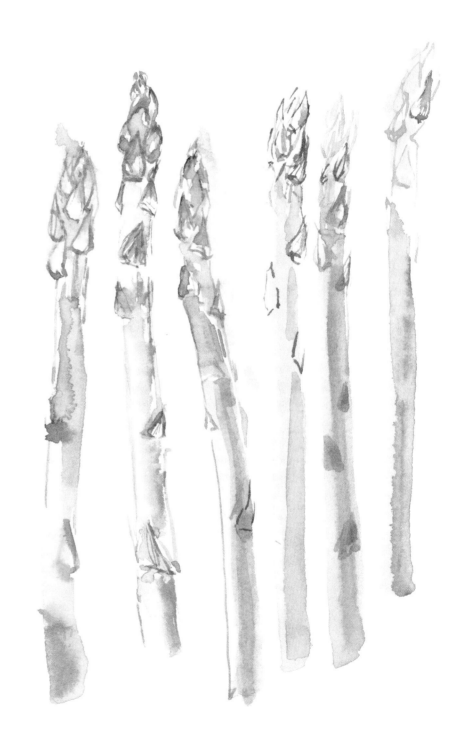

Brined pork loin *with* peas, artichokes *&* brown sage butter

SERVES 8

Brining the loin makes pork delicious to even the hardiest of pork naysayers. At the restaurant, diners have no choice about what they will be eating for lunch, and while we always ask if there is something that people don't eat, it's inevitable that some will fall through the reservation vetting system. More often than not, it's people who don't actually enjoy pork. The happy side of the story is that many will, albeit a little reluctantly, give pork cooked this way a go and, not surprisingly, they love it.

You'll need to make the brine at least one day before you want to serve this meal to allow plenty of time to make sure it's cold. I love to start the whole piece of loin on a chargrill or barbecue and then finish it in the oven. Mashed potato is the perfect base for this as it soaks up all the delicious brown sage butter.

———————————

To make the brine, bring 4 litres (135 fl oz) of water to the boil in a large saucepan along with all the other ingredients, then reduce the heat and simmer until the salt has dissolved. Set aside to cool. Add the loin in a whole piece and leave in the brine for 24 hours. Remove and pat dry.

Preheat the oven to 200°C (400°F).

Preheat a barbecue grill plate or chargrill pan until hot. Add the whole piece of loin and grill on all sides until it has lovely char lines up and down the length of it. Transfer to a roasting tin, then put in the oven and cook for 45 minutes or until the internal temperature reaches 70°C (150°F). Remove, cover with foil and set aside to rest while you prepare the vegetables.

1.6 kg (3½ lb) piece of pork loin (ask your butcher for the eye only, no skin or belly)
salt flakes and freshly ground black pepper
250 g (9 oz) shelled peas
1 kg (2 lb 3 oz) broad beans in the pod, podded
16 small cooked artichoke hearts (either bought ones or see page 144 for instructions on how to prepare your own)
200 g (7 oz) unsalted butter
1 quantity Mashed Potato (see page 206)
16 sage leaves

BRINE
125 g (4½ oz) salt flakes
180 g (6½ oz) honey
1 bay leaf
1 teaspoon peppercorns
2 thyme sprigs

Blanch the peas in a saucepan of boiling water for 5 minutes, then refresh in iced water. Drain and set aside.

Blanch the broad beans in a saucepan of boiling water for 3 minutes, then refresh in iced water. Drain and pop out of their outer skins.

Prepare the artichokes as directed on page 144 if you are using fresh ones.

Melt half the butter in a frying pan over a medium heat and warm the vegetables through for a couple of minutes.

While they are heating, carve the loin into thin slices.

Smear half the mashed potato on a warm platter, arrange the sliced pork on it, then spoon over the warmed vegetables. Return the pan to the heat, add the remaining butter and the sage leaves and cook over a high heat until the butter starts to brown. Sprinkle with a little pinch of salt flakes, then spoon the butter sauce over the meat and vegetables. Serve the remaining mashed potato on the side.

Orange puddings

SERVES 8

Oranges and Seville oranges are still about in surprising numbers in early to mid spring. In fact, I always make my year's supply of Seville orange marmalade in September, as this is when my former neighbour gives me my annual holler to come and get the oranges.

This is a curious little pudding that doesn't have any milk in it. It has a light, grainy sort of texture that I find very pleasing, and it sits beautifully on the plate with creme fraiche ice cream.

———————————

Preheat the oven to 160°C (320°F).

Butter and lightly flour eight 200 ml (7 fl oz) pudding moulds. (Don't be tempted to skip this step otherwise your puddings may stick.) Place a tablespoon of marmalade in each pudding mould and set aside.

Place the butter, brown sugar and caster sugar in a stand mixer fitted with the paddle attachment and beat until light and fluffy. Add the eggs, one at a time, then gently fold in the flour and orange zest and juice.

Divide the mixture evenly among the pudding moulds (the mixture should come two-thirds of the way up the moulds), then place on a large baking tray and bake for 40–45 minutes or until springy and golden.

170 g (6 oz) orange marmalade
240 g (8½ oz) unsalted butter
140 g (5 oz) soft brown sugar
140 g (5 oz) caster (superfine) sugar
4 eggs
240 g (8½ oz) self-raising flour
finely grated zest and juice of 1 orange

CREME FRAICHE ICE CREAM
500 ml (17 fl oz) milk
6 egg yolks
300 g (10½ oz) caster (superfine) sugar
250 ml (8½ fl oz) pouring (single/light) cream
300 g (10½ oz) creme fraiche
finely grated zest of 1 lemon

To make the creme fraiche ice cream, heat the milk in a saucepan and bring to scalding point. Whisk the egg yolks and sugar until pale, then pour in the hot milk and whisk until smooth and combined. Return the mixture to the saucepan and cook, stirring, over a medium heat until thickened. Remove from the heat and whisk in the cream, creme fraiche and lemon zest. Set aside to cool, then churn in an ice-cream machine according to the manufacturer's instructions.

Turn out the orange puddings onto individual plates and serve warm with a good scoop of creme fraiche ice cream.

TIMELINE

THE DAY BEFORE

Make the brine and chill.

Place the pork in the brine.

Make the creme fraiche ice cream.

THE DAY OF SERVING

Make the pastry.

Prepare the artichokes and refrigerate.

Hard-boil the eggs, shell and refrigerate.

Churn the ice cream.

Remove the pork from the brine and pat dry.

1—2 HOURS BEFORE SERVING

Roll out the pastry.

Prepare the asparagus.

Prepare the peas and broad beans.

Snip and cut all herbs, then refrigerate.

An hour before, chargrill and cook the pork loin, then cover with foil.

Assemble the asparagus tart.

Prepare the pudding moulds.

Make the pudding mixture.

Make the mashed potato.

TO SERVE

Cook the tart and grate the eggs over.

Scatter the tart with herbs and serve.

Warm the mash.

Return the pork (still in foil) to a 180°C (350°F) oven for 10 minutes to warm a little.

Fill the pudding moulds and arrange them on a tray.

When you remove the pork from the oven, turn the oven down and pop the puddings in.

Set a timer for the puddings.

Make the butter sauce for the pork.

Slice the pork and assemble the dish, to serve.

Remove the puddings from the oven and rest for a couple of minutes before turning out onto plates and serving with a scoop of ice cream.

The spring equinox is a special time of celebration. Don't forget that the Roman year started on the Ides of March, that in medieval England the year changed over in the last days of March, the Persian calendar started on the spring equinox, and Easter, Passover and other major religious festivals are tethered to the spring equinox. It is a time of rebirth. In my garden, the magic calendar turns over and all the fruit and vegetables that are to grace my table over the coming months start to thrive.

And it's a time for eggs, as a simple symbol of fertility and birth. In honour of this truly celebratory time I offer this very special menu which, naturally, includes eggs. Lots of eggs.

MENU THREE

MID – LATE SPRING	*Lunch or Dinner*

Steak tartare

Salade Lyonnaise

Suckling pig

Chocolate pot au creme *with*
salted caramel sauce *&* cinnamon brioche

Steak tartare

SERVES 8

This is truly one of my favourite things to eat and also one of my favourite food memories. As a young adolescent I was a very 'bad' eater, and one night my parents took me to a fancy restaurant. They didn't want a newly minted vile teenager there to help celebrate their anniversary, but it was unavoidable as they had failed to secure the services of a babysitter. Well I surprised us all that night, especially myself, by ordering steak tartare for my entree. 'Yes', I mumbled after both my parents and the kind waiter asked whether I knew it was raw meat. When it arrived – a beautifully sculpted pile of seasoned meat cradling a raw quail egg – it was like falling in love for the first time.

The beef is easier to hand-mince if it is very cold or even a bit frozen, so chill it in the freezer for an hour or so before you chop it. It is also best to cut the meat just before serving.

Preheat the oven to 200°C (400°F).

Slice the baguette very thinly on the diagonal and lay in a single layer on a baking tray. Bake for 10 minutes or until crisp. Remove and set aside to cool.

Hand-mince the meat by cutting it into the tiniest squares you possibly can.

Put all the condiments – the anchovy, shallot, capers, cornichons and parsley – in separate small bowls.

I like to serve tartare individually so people can add their own seasonings. Divide the meat into eight portions. Form each portion into a ball, then flatten it and put it on a plate. Make an indent in the centre and crack in a quail egg. Arrange little piles of each condiment on the plate next to the steak. Have worcestershire and tabasco sauce, mustard, olive oil, lemon wedges, salt and pepper on the table with a bowl of toasts. Encourage your guests to dig in and mix their own tartare.

1 Baguette (see page 204)

700 g (1 lb 9 oz) beef eye fillet, trimmed of all sinew and fat

8 Ortiz anchovy fillets, mashed with the flat edge of a knife

8 French shallots, finely diced

1 tablespoon small salted capers, rinsed and squeezed dry

8 cornichons, finely diced

1¼ tablespoons finely chopped flat-leaf (Italian) parsley

8 quail eggs

worcestershire sauce, tabasco sauce, dijon mustard and extra-virgin olive oil, to serve

8 lemon wedges

salt flakes and freshly ground black pepper

Salade Lyonnaise

SERVES 8

Again, it's all about the egg, only it's softly poached this time.
This classic French salad really doesn't need an introduction.

———————————————

Wash and separate the frisee into manageable pieces. Drain.

Heat a heavy-based frying pan over a high heat, add the clarified
butter and heat until quite hot. Add the bread cubes and toss until
they start to become golden. Add the bacon and continue tossing
until the croutes are golden brown and crisp and the bacon is
cooked. Lift out with a slotted spoon and place in a bowl, reserving
the bacon fat.

In a mixing bowl, whisk together the oil, vinegar, bacon fat and
shallot.

Season a medium saucepan of water with salt and a dash of vinegar
and bring to the boil. Break the eggs into a clean bowl, make a
whirlpool in the boiling water and pour in the eggs. Bring back to
a simmer and poach for 5 minutes or until soft. Gently lift out the
poached eggs with a slotted spoon and drain on a tray or plate
lined with paper towel.

Place the frisee in a large mixing bowl with the herbs, bacon,
croutes and dressing. Toss until well combined and coated in
the dressing. Pile onto a serving platter, top with the drained
poached eggs and serve.

2 frisee lettuces

100 g (3½ oz) clarified butter

4 slices French or Italian bread, crusts
    removed, cut into 1 cm (½ in) cubes

4 rindless rashers bacon, cut into lardons

120 ml (4 fl oz) extra-virgin olive oil

120 ml (4 fl oz) white wine vinegar

1 tablespoon finely chopped French shallots

salt flakes and freshly ground black pepper

dash of white vinegar

8 eggs

1 tablespoon each of snipped chives, flat-leaf
    (Italian) parsley and chervil

Suckling pig

SERVES 8

Now, just because I have been alluding to the great pagan festivities of times gone by, I'm not going to start a recipe with 'First, sacrifice your piglet'. But serving a whole suckling pig reminds us all that meat is a life: a life that has been taken for our enjoyment and for our sustenance, a life that should never be taken for granted. This is a dish that requires your utmost respect as you cook and serve it.

Traditionally, a whole suckling pig would be cooked on a spit, either twirling over hot coals or on a proper French rotisserie, dripping its fat onto a pan of potatoes below. Neither of these items are terribly handy around the home. The next problem is that most 60 cm (24 in) ovens will be unable to fit a whole pig. If you have a 90 cm (35 ½ in) oven it is possible to cook an 8 kg (17 lb 12 oz) whole pig, but if you have a small oven it's best to purchase a quarter of a larger suckling pig. I will give the recipe for a quarter – it's not as dramatic as the whole little pig, but is equally delicious. And I must pay homage to MoVida's Frank Camorra, as it's a Spaniard I turned to for advice when I first started roasting suckling pigs. They know a thing or two about pigs, the Spanish.

This goes beautifully with Roasted Potatoes (see page 206), blanched spring greens (see page 206) and a fresh green salad.

Preheat the oven to 220°C (430°F).

Choose a large flameproof baking dish that will accommodate the pig. Pour in the vinegar and 1 litre (34 fl oz) of water, add the bay leaves and half the thyme and bring to the boil. Place the pig in the dish, skin side down, and boil for 90 seconds, then turn it over and cook for another 90 seconds. Remove the meat, discarding the cooking liquid, and pat the meat dry. Allow to dry at room temperature for at least 30 minutes.

500 ml (17 fl oz) white vinegar
4 bay leaves
1 bunch thyme
the hind or the forequarter of a 15–20 kg
    (33–44 lb) suckling pig
1 garlic bulb, halved horizontally
3 carrots, roughly chopped
3 onions, roughly chopped
salt flakes
extra-virgin olive oil, for drizzling

Place the garlic, carrot and onion in the bottom of the baking dish. Season the pork on both sides with salt, drizzle with a little olive oil and then massage in the salt. Put the dish in the oven and roast for 45–50 minutes or until the skin is golden and crisp. Turn the oven down to 160°C (320°F) and cook for another 30 minutes. Remove and rest for 10 minutes, then transfer to a serving platter. Carve at the table.

Chocolate pot au creme *with* salted caramel sauce *&* cinnamon brioche

SERVES 8

I did say there would be a lot of eggs in this menu. And it doesn't get more eggy than custard and brioche, that great celebration bread. Personally, I like to set my pot au creme and serve my salted caramel in individual 100 ml (3½ fl oz) jam jars, but not everyone has 16 small jars in their kitchen; instead, you can cook the custards in little souffle dishes or make one large bowl of custard and salted caramel and plonk them in the middle of the table to share.

Preheat the oven to 160°C (320°F).

To make the chocolate pot au creme, combine the cream, milk, sugar and vanilla in a heavy-based saucepan over a medium heat. Bring to the boil, whisking gently as the mixture heats. When it is boiling, add the chocolate and whisk until the chocolate has melted and the mixture is smooth. Remove from the heat and set aside to cool a little.

In a bowl, lightly beat the egg yolks and then gradually pour into the chocolate mixture, whisking gently. Strain the mixture into a jug and pour into your chosen dishes. Place these in a roasting tin lined with a tea towel and pour boiling water into the tin to come halfway up the side of the dishes. Cover the tin with foil and bake for 45 minutes or until the custards are just set with a slight wobble in the middle. If you are using small moulds, check after 25 minutes.

Remove the chocolate pots from the roasting tin and refrigerate until ready to serve.

To make the brioche dough, combine the flour and salt in the bowl of a stand mixer fitted with the paddle attachment. Heat the milk until lukewarm, then add the yeast and sugar and stir to dissolve. Add the egg yolks and whisk together. Gradually pour the liquid into the mixer bowl, beating constantly. Beat for 5 minutes on a moderate

300 ml (10 fl oz) pouring
    (single/light) cream
unsalted butter, to serve
¼ teaspoon ground cinnamon mixed
    with 2 tablespoons raw sugar
1 quantity Salted Caramel Sauce
    (see page 32)

CHOCOLATE POT AU CREME
375 ml (12½ fl oz) pouring
    (single/light) cream
250 ml (8½ fl oz) milk
110 g (4 oz) caster (superfine) sugar
1 teaspoon natural vanilla extract
250 g (9 oz) dark (55%) chocolate,
    chopped or in buttons
6 egg yolks

BRIOCHE DOUGH
500 g (1 lb 2 oz) plain (all-purpose) flour
1 teaspoon salt flakes
250 ml (8½ fl oz) milk
2 teaspoons instant dried yeast
40 g (1½ oz) caster (superfine) sugar
6 egg yolks
150 g (5½ oz) soft unsalted butter,
    cut into cubes

speed, then increase the speed and add the butter bit by
bit – by now the paddle will be slapping the dough quite
vigorously, which is what you want. It should come away from
the side of the bowl during this process.

Place the dough in a clean bowl, then cover with plastic wrap
and allow to rise in a warm place for 2 hours or until more than
doubled in size.

Grease two standard loaf tins. Punch down the dough and turn
it out onto a work surface. Cut it in half and form each portion
into a rectangle. Place in the tins and set aside to prove for
another 30 minutes.

Preheat the oven to 210°C (410°F).

Place the loaf tins in the oven and cook for 10 minutes, then
reduce the temperature to 180°C (350°F) and cook for a further
15–20 minutes. Remove the brioche loaves from the tins and cool
on a wire rack.

Just before you're ready to serve, whip the cream to soft peaks.

Slice the brioche and toast it, then spread with butter
and sprinkle with the cinnamon sugar.

Serve the toasted brioche with the pot au creme,
caramel sauce and whipped cream.

TIMELINE

THE DAY BEFORE

Make the chocolate pot au creme and refrigerate.

Prepare the brioche.

Make the caramel sauce.

THE DAY OF SERVING

Prepare all the condiments for the tartare and refrigerate.

Make the melba toast.

Wash the lettuce.

Make the Lyonnaise dressing.

Prepare the salad and vegetables for the suckling pig.

1–2 HOURS BEFORE SERVING

Prepare and start to roast the pig.

Whip the cream.

TO SERVE

The pig should be about ready when you serve the tartare so turn the oven down.

Put the potatoes in the low oven – you can turn it up later when you rest the pig.

Chop the steak and serve the tartare.

Fry the croutes and bacon, poach the eggs and assemble the salad.

Remove the pig from the oven.

Increase the temperature to 220°C (430°F) to finish off the potatoes.

Serve the Salade Lyonnaise.

Arrange the pig on a platter and take to the table for carving.

Serve the pig with the salad, greens and potatoes. Turn the oven to low.

Toast the brioche, butter it and sprinkle with cinnamon sugar. Keep it warm in a low oven while you toast all the slices.

Arrange your chocolate custard, cream, caramel sauce and toast so that you and your guests can liberally spread their toast with 'goodness'.

A happy menu, full of the joys of spring. I serve this right at the end of spring, on the cusp of those often faltering first days of summer. There is something incredibly beautiful about this time of year: the roses are out, the fruit trees are blossoming, everything is green and there is the most wonderful sense of abundance. And to my eye, my house, my garden and my restaurant are all at their absolute peak. Each season has its difficult moments and its perfect moments, but if I could pick a moment in time across the whole year where I would like time to stand still, it would be a late spring morning. I love this time of year with an absolute passion, and this little menu embodies the sense of whimsy that these days bring.

MENU FOUR

LATE SPRING	*Lunch or Dinner*

Artichoke pies

Rack *of* lamb *with* peas,
broad beans *&* spring herbs

Strawberry *&* raspberry roulade

Artichoke pies

SERVES 8

This recipe started its life in my friend Phillippa Grogan's book, *Phillippa's Home Baking*. I was searching for what I could possibly do with hundreds of the last tiny artichokes of the season. Phillippa's pie seemed like a godsend, and it was. I've tweaked the recipe here and there to suit my kitchen and really look forward to making it every year.

———————————

First, prepare your artichokes. Have on hand a container of cold water which will hold the prepared artichokes. Put one of the cut lemons in the water.

Pull off the outer leaves of the artichokes until you get down to the paler green and yellow leaves. Cut the stem to about 3 cm (1¼ in) long, then cut about two-thirds off the top of the flower part and discard. Cut the trimmed artichoke in half and scoop out the 'choke' with a teaspoon. Rub with the cut lemon to prevent it from browning, then place in the container of water. Continue until you finish all the artichokes.

Pour the oil, wine and 120 ml (4 fl oz) water into a saucepan and add the onion and carrot. Bring to the boil, then reduce the heat and simmer for 10 minutes. Add the artichokes and cook for about 7 minutes or until the artichokes are tender. Remove from the heat. The artichokes can be stored like this in the refrigerator for a couple of weeks as long as they are submerged in the liquid.

Grease a standard 12-hole muffin tin. (This recipe makes 12 pies, giving you four extra, either for greedy people at your dinner or to be enjoyed another day.) Roll out the pastry to a 2 mm (1/16 in) thickness and cut out circles to fit into the muffin holes. The pastry base should extend over the top of the tin by about 1 cm (½ in) and the lids should be cut to fit the top of the muffin holes. Place the muffin tin in the refrigerator and the lids on a plate, also in the refrigerator.

6–8 medium–large, tight globe artichokes
2 lemons, halved
100 ml (3½ fl oz) olive oil
100 ml (3½ fl oz) white wine
1 onion, thinly sliced
1 carrot, thinly sliced on the diagonal
1 quantity Kate's Excellent Shortcrust Pastry (see page 208)
200 g (7 oz) fresh ricotta
75 g (2¾ oz) freshly grated parmesan
2 eggs
salt flakes and freshly ground black pepper
200 g (7 oz) small salad leaves

SHERRY VINAIGRETTE
100 ml (3½ fl oz) sherry vinegar
100 ml (3½ fl oz) extra-virgin olive oil
200 ml (7 fl oz) grapeseed oil
salt flakes and freshly ground black pepper

Drain the artichokes, cut each half into four and place in a bowl. Mix in the ricotta, parmesan and one egg, and season to taste with salt and pepper. Remove the muffin tin from the refrigerator and fill each of the pastry bases with the artichoke mixture. Whisk the remaining egg to make an egg wash. Paint the underside of the lids with egg wash, then place on top of pies. Pinch the pastry base and lid together and then roll over to form a pretty edge. Refrigerate for at least 15 minutes or until you are ready to cook them.

Preheat the oven to 220°C (430°F).

Bake the pies for 10–15 minutes or until golden brown.

To make the sherry vinaigrette, whisk together the vinegar and oils, then season with a little salt and pepper. Toss about 100 ml (3½ fl oz) of the dressing with the salad leaves. This makes more dressing than you'll need but it's good to have in the refrigerator as your 'house vinaigrette', and it pops up again in the next recipe.

Carefully unmould the pies from the tin and serve with a little dressed salad.

Rack *of* lamb *with* peas, broad beans *&* spring herbs

SERVES 8

As a good Australian girl, I have to feature a spring lamb dish. Lamb has become quite a luxury meat, and this dish is no exception. It is a perfect case of savouring and appreciating a small serving of meat rather than viewing it as a massive filler on the plate; this is probably why I start this menu with a good gutsy pie. What I offer here is a delicate rack of lamb, served with spring herbs, spring greens, croutes baked in olive oil and garlic, a little dressing and a drizzle of enriched pan juices.

_____

Preheat the oven to 200°C (400°F).

Trim any excess fat from the lamb racks. Cut small slits in the top of the lamb with a small, sharp knife, then insert small pieces of rosemary and half the garlic slices into the slits. Set the lamb aside.

Cut the bread into rough 1 cm (½ in) cubes and toss in a little olive oil and the remaining garlic. Scatter over a baking tray and toast in the oven for 10 minutes or until golden brown, tossing halfway through. Remove from the oven.

Meanwhile, mix all the chopped herbs together and set aside.

Put the lamb racks in a baking dish and bake for 20 minutes until medium–rare or until cooked to your liking.

Remove from the oven and rest, covered, in a warm place for 10 minutes to allow the juices to be absorbed back into the meat.

8 lamb racks (with 3 cutlets per rack)
2 rosemary sprigs
8 garlic cloves, sliced
8 slices sourdough bread
olive oil, for tossing
2 teaspoons chopped chervil
2 teaspoons chopped flat-leaf
   (Italian) parsley
2 teaspoons snipped chives
400 g (14 oz) shelled peas
200 g (7 oz) podded and peeled broad beans
250 g (9 oz) rocket (arugula) leaves
100 ml (3½ fl oz) Sherry Vinaigrette
   (see page 144)
salt flakes

Bring a saucepan of salted water to the boil, add the peas and cook until just tender – this should only take a couple of minutes, depending on size. At the last minute, drop in the broad beans to just warm through. Drain well.

Toss together the rocket, herbs and croutes in a bowl and sprinkle with the dressing and a little salt. Place on a big platter, then scatter over the peas and broad beans. Cut the lamb into individual cutlets, arrange the cutlets on the salad and pour over any juices left in the baking dish.

Strawberry & raspberry roulade

SERVES 8

I would never have thought I would gravitate towards pretty pink desserts, but I do. I seem to have quite a repertoire of them. This is one of my favourites – fancy, yet frivolous, and dead simple to make and execute. Meringue roulades are lovely things, and they are excellent for using up extra egg whites. This one has new-season raspberries and sweet, juicy spring strawberries, bound together with lashings of cream. Rolled, sculpted, decorated and served with a flourish at the table, this dessert always makes my restaurant customers smile. It makes me smile too, and explains without words why I love this time of year so, so much.

4 egg whites

250 g (9 oz) caster (superfine) sugar, plus extra for dusting

1 teaspoon white wine vinegar

1 teaspoon cornflour (cornstarch)

300 ml (10 fl oz) thick (double/heavy) cream

225 g (8 oz) strawberries, hulled and quartered if large

200 g (7 oz) raspberries

Preheat the oven to 190°C (375°F). Grease and line a 33 x 23 cm (13 x 9 in) Swiss roll tin (jelly roll tin) with baking paper.

Place the egg whites in the bowl of a stand mixer fitted with the whisk attachment and whisk until thick. Whisk in the sugar, one-third at a time, then fold in the vinegar and cornflour.

Spoon the meringue into the prepared tin and smooth the surface. Bake for 10 minutes, then reduce the oven temperature to 160°C (320°F) and cook for a further 5 minutes.

Place a clean tea towel on the benchtop, cover with a sheet of baking paper and sprinkle with extra caster sugar. Turn out the meringue onto the baking paper and set aside to cool for 1–2 hours.

Whip the cream, then spread most of it over the cooled meringue, keeping about one-quarter aside for decoration. Scatter the strawberries and raspberries over the cream, reserving a few strawberries for decoration.

Use the tea towel to gently but firmly roll up the roulade. Carefully transfer it to a long platter, then pipe the reserved cream in a long pattern down the length of the roulade. Decorate with the reserved strawberries and serve.

TIMELINE

THE DAY OF SERVING

Make the pastry and refrigerate.

Prepare the artichokes.

Make the dressing.

Clean the salad leaves and refrigerate.

Make the meringue for the roulade.

Roll out the pastry for the pies and refrigerate.

Assemble the pies.

1–2 HOURS BEFORE SERVING

Prepare the lamb racks.

Cut the croutes.

Prepare the vegetables and herbs.

Wash the rocket.

Whip the cream.

Assemble the roulade (except the fruit decoration) and refrigerate.

TO SERVE

Cook the pies and serve.

Once you take the pies out of the oven, reduce the temperature and place the lamb racks in.

Set a timer for the lamb.

Remove and rest the lamb racks.

Assemble the lamb 'salad' and arrange on a platter to serve.

Finish decorating the roulade with the fruit and serve.

SUMMER

SUMMER

In my little world, summer days exist in three parts: the cool of the morning, the respite of the evening, and the long bit in the middle. Most of the blazingly hot middle part of the day is spent in the kitchen. It doesn't seem to matter what's going on outside, a restaurant kitchen is always hot in the summer. And I actually don't mind this; the sweat and the toil make me feel really alive.

The cool of the morning is the most wondrous part of the day. Tommy and I walk daily down a meandering path that rarely changes. For most of the year we walk so early that it's still dark, but for the duration of summer we get to actually see where we are walking. The little village of Malmsbury is an old settlement in Australian terms. It is a tiny town with extraordinary evidence of man's strength, ingenuity and vision: an amazing multi-arched bluestone railway bridge, an old botanic garden where Europe still tries to flourish in the antipodes, and a water reservoir with a dam wall of bluestone cut and laid entirely by hand. I often think of the men, long-since dead, who created this legacy. I wonder how harsh the world would have been for them, and why they saw Malmsbury as such a promising site when now, 150 years later, it is a tiny hamlet, quietly existing among the grandeur of its structures. It's a beautiful walk, and a quiet time to reflect on what the new day will bring. Once home, Tommy and I busy ourselves in the garden, picking and sorting fruit and vegetables for the day, before the relentless heat descends and picking anything becomes a waste of time.

The evenings are devoted to watering – watering everyone and everything. Those big cats, Fenn and Kitten, appear from wherever they have been hiding from the heat, and chase and tumble and fight as I drag the hose from one garden bed to the next. When they've finished their boisterous routine, Kitten will usually assume his position on my shoulder to get a bird's eye view of the world and Fenn will roll endlessly in the loose gravel of the paths, scratching his back on the grit. Tommy trots up and down the paths, looking for lizards or vermin that may be silly enough to come out for an evening stroll while he is on patrol.

Sometimes, during those long, languid summer nights, I wish my world was a little different. If only it were possible to pick up my restaurant and put it in my garden. I can think of nothing nicer than starting a long casual evening of feasting as the sun begins to set in the western sky. A barbecue, a wood-fired oven, a long table set and ready for company. Plenty of Champagne, beer and chilled rose. And glorious platters of simple food, whether it be French farmhouse or something a long-gone quarry master might have eaten. Some say that food is simply the fuel that we need to survive. But who wants to go to all that trouble just to survive? Good food and the joy of cooking is all about the pursuit of love – the love of friends and family and those you strive to make happy.

The menus at du Fermier follow a familiar pattern. I work out which vegetables are ready in the garden and then I match a protein to them. There is no doubt that there are some favourites in my repertoire, and it leads to some unashamed repeats of dishes and menus.

In my opinion, the greatest misconception about cooking from recipes is that they will always work perfectly. Preparing good food often takes practice, lots of practice, and I've found as I've grown older that there is no shame in finding a recipe or technique that you are comfortable with and using it as a basis for different culinary creations across the seasons. This menu features pork and pastry that I've used before, but different ingredients and garnishes illustrate the joy of mastering a technique and adapting it to seasonal produce when it's at its best.

MENU ONE

EARLY SUMMER	*Lunch or Dinner*

French breakfast radishes & butter

Spaghetti *with* zucchini, garlic,
anchovy & olive oil

Barbecued brined pork loin
with summer slaw & mashed potato

Peaches baked *in* puff *with* vanilla custard

French breakfast radishes & butter

SERVES 8

For years now I have been growing and serving little French breakfast radishes as hors d'oeuvres. They are delicious, peppery morsels, and you certainly don't need to mess with them. Good butter and good salt are all you need.

2 bunches French breakfast radishes
50 g (1¾ oz) unsalted butter, softened
1 teaspoon salt flakes

Trim the excess greenery from the top of the radishes, then wash them well and pat dry with paper towel.

Serve prettily on a platter with the butter and a pile of salt flakes.

Spaghetti *with* zucchini, garlic, anchovy *&* olive oil

SERVES 8

One of the eternal questions of summer is how to use up all the zucchini. Even if you don't grow it yourself, I am sure many loving friends will kindly bestow their excess on you. If it doesn't sound too pushy, encourage them to pick them small and young for you (under 8 cm/3 ¼ in), then invite them over for this amazing pasta dish.

Bring a large saucepan of salted water to the boil.

While the water is heating, run the zucchini through the julienne blades of a mandoline. If you don't have a mandoline, use a vegetable peeler to shave off ribbons, then cut them as finely as you can into thin strips.

Crush the garlic and then the anchovies with the back of a knife and set aside.

Place the spaghetti in the boiling water and cook according to the packet instructions until al dente (for spaghetti it's usually 10–12 minutes).

Warm the olive oil in a large frying pan over a low heat, add the garlic and anchovy and swirl it around to soften (you don't want the garlic to burn or it will be bitter). Add the zucchini and cook for about 5 minutes.

Drain the spaghetti, add to the zucchini mixture and toss together. Season to taste with salt and pepper. Divide among individual bowls, or one big platter, and shave the parmesan over the top. Serve immediately.

4 medium or 8 small zucchini (courgettes)
2 garlic cloves
4 Ortiz anchovies
750 g (1 lb 1 oz) good-quality
  dried spaghetti
160 ml (5½ fl oz) extra-virgin olive oil
salt flakes and freshly ground black pepper
80 g (2¾ oz) Grana Padano or other
  good-quality parmesan

Barbecued brined pork loin *with* summer slaw *&* mashed potato

SERVES 8

This uses the same cut of meat and cooking method as the pork loin in the Spring chapter. This way of cooking pork is an absolute winner and, in the heat of summer, it can be rested, sliced very thinly and served at room temperature. The mash soaks up the meat juices, sweetened by the brine, and the slaw gives a sharp crunch counterpoint. Don't forget the pork needs to brine for 24 hours, so start this recipe at least a day before you wish to serve it.

―――――――――――

Add the loin to the brine in a whole piece and leave for 24 hours. Remove and pat dry.

Preheat the oven to 200°C (400°F).

Preheat a barbecue grill plate or chargrill pan until hot. Add the whole piece of loin and grill on all sides until it has lovely char lines up and down the length of it. Transfer to a roasting tin, then put in the oven and cook for 45 minutes or until the internal temperature reads 70°C (150°F). Remove, cover with foil and set aside to rest while you prepare the slaw.

To make the summer slaw, it's best to have a mandoline slicer; if not, do your best with a very sharp knife. Slice the beetroot very thinly, and then cut into thin julienne strips. Shred the cabbage very finely, then slice the onion very thinly. Place all the vegetables in a mixing bowl. Combine the creme fraiche, oil and vinegar in a small bowl, then mix through the vegetables and season to taste. Decorate with chervil sprigs and capers.

To serve, place the mashed potato on the bottom of a platter. Slice the meat very thinly and add to the platter, then pour over the juices that have collected under the resting meat. Serve with the summer slaw.

1.6 kg (3½ lb) piece of pork loin (ask your butcher for the eye only, no skin or belly)
1 quantity Brine (see page 124)
1 quantity Mashed Potato (see page 206)

SUMMER SLAW
2 beetroots, peeled
½ red cabbage
1 small red onion
200 g (7 oz) creme fraiche
50 ml (1¾ fl oz) extra-virgin olive oil
50 ml (1¾ fl oz) Forum cabernet vinegar or other good-quality red wine vinegar
salt flakes and freshly ground black pepper
½ bunch chervil, picked into little sprigs
1 tablespoon small salted capers, rinsed and squeezed dry

Peaches baked *in* puff *with* vanilla custard

SERVES 8

I can't help myself when it comes to fruit and puff pastry tarts; they are so delicious and so French. An old French woman once told me she didn't understand our obsession with removing pits and stones from things, and this has stayed with me. At the restaurant, I cook the whole peach in the tart, counting on the diners' common sense to eat around the stone.

This is the perfect finish to a summer meal, especially if you have a little vanilla ice cream tucked away in your freezer.

Preheat the oven to 210°C (410°F) and line a large baking tray with baking paper.

Combine the sugar with 1 litre (34 fl oz) of water and the vanilla bean in a large saucepan and bring to the boil, stirring to dissolve the sugar. Reduce to a simmer and carefully add the peaches. Simmer for 5 minutes, then remove with a slotted spoon and plunge into a bowl of iced water (reserve the sugar syrup). Gently slip the skins from the fruit and place the peaches on a plate to drain.

Roll out the puff pastry to a thickness of about 5 mm (¼ in). Cut out eight circles that are 2 cm (¾ in) larger than the peaches.

Place the pastry discs on the prepared tray and top each one with a peach (reserve the last two peaches for later). Bake for 10 minutes, then reduce the oven temperature to 180°C (350°F) and bake for a further 10–15 minutes or until the pastry is golden brown. Remove from the oven and place on a wire rack.

While the pastries are cooking, remove the stones from the reserved peaches and puree the flesh with a little of the reserved sugar syrup to make a sauce.

1 kg (2 lb 3 oz) granulated sugar
1 vanilla bean, split lengthways
  and seeds scraped
10 perfectly ripe yellow or white
  free-stone peaches
1 quantity Puff Pastry (see page 209)
good-quality vanilla ice cream,
  to serve (optional)

VANILLA CUSTARD
500 ml (17 fl oz) pouring
  (single/light) cream
½ vanilla bean, split lengthways
  and seeds scraped
6 egg yolks
125 g (4½ oz) caster (superfine) sugar

To make the vanilla custard, pour the cream into a saucepan, add the vanilla and bring to scalding point. Whisk the egg yolks and sugar until pale. Pour the hot milk onto the yolk mixture and whisk together until smooth. Return to the cleaned saucepan and cook, stirring, over a medium heat until thickened. Remove from the heat and strain into a jug.

Serve the peach pastries with the sauce, custard and a spoonful of vanilla ice cream, if you like.

TIMELINE

THE DAY BEFORE

Prepare the brine and chill.

Brine the pork.

Make the puff pastry.

THE DAY OF SERVING

Roll and cut the pastry.

Prepare the peaches.

Make the custard.

Make the peach sauce.

Prepare the slaw, but don't dress it.

I—2 HOURS BEFORE SERVING

Prepare the radishes.

Prepare the vegetables for the pasta.

Make the mashed potato.

TO SERVE

Cook the pork loin.

Plate and serve the radishes.

Remove the pork from the oven and rest.

Cook and serve the spaghetti.

Warm the mashed potato.

Slice the meat.

Dress the slaw and serve the sliced pork and mash.

Increase the oven temperature to 210°C (410°F).

Once the mains are cleared, cook the peach tarts, then serve with sauce, custard and ice cream.

Summer sets in and the heat starts to creep through everything, everywhere. The cats become languid, lazing about the farm doing little or nothing at all. Kitten tends to hide in the soft, cool fern forest that the asparagus turns into, lazily poking at the odd skink that makes the mistake of running within a paw's reach. Fenn abandons his usual pursuit of hunting and finds cool places to lie, on the concrete under the laundry trough or, when it's terribly hot, you can find him stretched full length in the cool metal of the tractor bucket.

My response to the weather is a menu of classic salads and light flavours – things that can be grazed on over a long, hot afternoon.

MENU TWO

EARLY — MID SUMMER	*Lunch or Dinner*

Pissaladiere

Salade nicoise *with* escalope *of* ocean trout

Lamb rump *with* rocket, cucumber,
minted yoghurt *&* roasted new potatoes

Vacherin *with* summer berries

Pissaladiere

SERVES 8

This take on the classic Provencale slice has the caramelised onions, anchovies and olives on a pastry base. It is traditionally made on a bread dough but I prefer the crunch and flake of pastry. Wherever you are, these evocative flavours will take you to Provence.

_____

Heat the oil in a large heavy-based saucepan over a high heat, add the onion and cook for about 10 minutes, stirring occasionally to make sure it doesn't catch.

Add the tomato and thyme and stir through, then cover and cook for 45 minutes, stirring occasionally. Remove from the heat and season to taste. Set aside to cool, then refrigerate.

Preheat the oven to 200°C (400°F). Line a 33 x 23 cm (13 x 9 in) baking tray with baking paper.

Roll out the pastry on a lightly floured surface to a thickness of about 3 mm (⅛ in). Fully line the prepared tray with pastry, cutting it slightly bigger than the tray so you have a little excess pastry to make a pretty rolled edge.

Spread the cold onion mixture over the pastry. Cut the anchovies in half lengthways and make a diamond-shaped grid pattern over the onion. Place half an olive inside each diamond.

Bake for 25 minutes or until golden brown. This can be eaten hot, warm, cold or even reheated. Cut into fingers or squares for serving.

50 ml (1¾ fl oz) olive oil

1 kg (2 lb 3 oz) brown onions, very thinly sliced

2 tomatoes, diced

2 thyme sprigs

salt flakes and freshly ground black pepper

1 quantity Kate's Excellent Shortcrust Pastry (see page 208)

47.5 g (about 1¾ oz) tin Ortiz anchovies

10 large black olives, halved and pitted if you wish

Salade nicoise *with* escalope *of* ocean trout

SERVES 8

Each and every year I feature a nicoise on my summer menu because it takes advantage of all the best summer produce I grow: tiny tomatoes, delicate little beans, newest of new potatoes and bantam eggs from the henhouse.

Nicoise is traditionally made with tuna, but I love serving it with ocean trout, cut into thin escalopes and briefly seared on one side only. This salad works equally well as a shared platter or as an assembled dish.

———————————

The first thing to do is to cut the trout into flat slices. To do this, put the flat of your hand on the end of the fish fillet, place the knife about 8 cm (3¼ in) from your hand and slice on an angle towards your hand. You're looking to create 5 mm (¼ in) thick slices about 8 cm (3¼ in) long and the width of the fish.

To make the dressing, whisk together the vinegar, oils and garlic. Set aside.

Place the potatoes in a saucepan, cover with cold water and add a large pinch of salt. Bring to the boil, then reduce the heat and simmer for about 20 minutes or until tender. Drain and set aside.

Meanwhile, bring a saucepan of water to the boil and cook the beans for 4–5 minutes. Drain, then refresh under cold running water or in a bowl of iced water, then drain again.

Just before you want to serve the salad, place a large non-stick frying pan over a high heat, or preheat the flat grill of a barbecue until hot.

800 g (1 lb 12 oz) ocean trout fillet, skin and bones removed
600 g (1 lb 5 oz) small waxy yellow potatoes (such as nicola), washed
salt flakes and freshly ground black pepper
250 g (9 oz) small green beans, topped and tailed
500 g (1 lb 2 oz) mixed cherry tomatoes, halved if large
150 g (5½ oz) ligurian olives
300 g (10½ oz) mixed salad greens
4 hard-boiled bantam or small eggs
47.5 g (about 1¾ oz) tin Ortiz anchovies
6 chives

DRESSING
50 ml (1¾ fl oz) sherry vinegar
50 ml (1¾ fl oz) extra-virgin olive oil
100 ml (3½ fl oz) grapeseed oil
1 garlic clove, crushed

Toss the potatoes, beans, cherry tomatoes and olives in a bowl with some of the dressing and a little salt and pepper. Place half the lettuce on a large platter, scatter over the potato mixture, then add the remaining salad leaves to give it some height.

Lightly oil and season the fish, then cook on one side only for 1 minute. Arrange over the salad. Cut the eggs in half and arrange on the salad, then decorate with strips of anchovy. Sprinkle more dressing over the completed salad, snip the chives over the top and serve.

Lamb rump *with* rocket, cucumber, minted yoghurt *&* roasted new potatoes

SERVES 8

While there is always a surplus of zucchini in summer, there is often an equal bounty of cucumbers. In the warmer months there are plenty of ways to use them: cold cucumber soup, lovely cucumber and crab salads, cucumber and smoked trout and, as here, paired with grilled lamb rump and minted yoghurt. This is a very simple dish to prepare. One lamb rump does just over one person, so six is more than adequate to serve eight.

_____

Place the potatoes in a large saucepan and cover with cold water. Bring to the boil, then reduce the heat and simmer for about 20 minutes or until just tender. Drain.

Meanwhile, preheat the oven to 200°C (400°F).

Cut the potatoes in half or into quarters, depending on their size, and toss with the thyme, salt, pepper and enough oil to lightly coat. Place in a roasting tin and roast for 25 minutes or until golden.

To make minted yoghurt, combine the yoghurt, garlic, lemon juice and mint in a bowl.

Preheat your barbecue until hot or place a chargrill pan over a high heat. (If you don't have either of these, just use a heavy-based frying pan.)

Season the lamb rumps generously with salt and pepper and lightly coat with oil. Place on the barbecue and cook for about 20 minutes, depending on the strength of your barbecue, turning every 5 minutes or so. If you are cooking the lamb on the stovetop, either mark them all over in a chargrill pan or seal them in a frying pan for about 10 minutes.

750 g (1 lb 10 oz) new potatoes, washed
4 thyme sprigs
salt flakes and freshly ground black pepper
olive oil, for cooking
6 lamb rumps
200 g (7 oz) rocket (arugula)
4 Lebanese (short) cucumbers, cut into
  8 mm (3/8 in) dice

MINTED YOGHURT
375 g (13 oz) Greek-style yoghurt
1 garlic clove, crushed
juice of 1/2 lemon
1 small handful of mint leaves,
  very thinly sliced

Transfer them to the oven and cook for a further 10–15 minutes, depending on whether you want rare or medium–rare. Remove from the oven, then cover loosely with foil and rest for 15–20 minutes.

To serve, arrange the rocket on a platter and scatter with the cucumber. Cut the meat into 5 mm (¼ in) thick slices and arrange over the salad, then pour over the meat resting juices. Either spread the minted yoghurt down the middle of the meat or serve in a separate bowl, along with the roasted new potatoes.

Vacherin *with* summer berries

SERVES 8

Summer really isn't complete without a showing of meringue, berries and cream. A vacherin can be plated in many different ways, but I love it in its classic form of a meringue shell filled with berries and cream. The little shells will keep quite happily in an airtight container up to five days – if you are layering them, I always find it best to put a piece of baking paper between each layer.

Preheat the oven to 140°C (275°F). Grease and line a large baking tray with baking paper.

Using a stand mixer fitted with the whisk attachment, beat the egg whites until really stiff peaks form. Add the caster sugar quickly and beat it in, then add the vanilla, vinegar and cornflour.

Spoon the meringue into a piping bag fitted with a 1 cm (½ in) star nozzle. Pipe eight 7 cm (2¾ in) discs on the prepared tray. Pipe a lip around the outer edge of each disc, then pipe another circle on the lip to create a shell that you can fill. Place the tray in the oven, reduce the temperature to 80°C (175°F) and cook for 1 hour. Remove from the oven and rest for 10 minutes, then transfer the meringues to a wire rack to cool.

While the meringues are cooking, whip the cream, hull the strawberries and inspect the other berries, discarding any that don't pass muster.

Shortly before serving, fill the shells two-thirds of the way with cream, then scatter the berries over the top. Dust with icing sugar and serve.

4 egg whites
250 g (9 oz) caster (superfine) sugar
a few drops of natural vanilla extract
1 teaspoon white vinegar
2 teaspoons cornflour (cornstarch)
300 ml (10 fl oz) thickened (whipping) cream
375 g (13 oz) mixed summer berries (such as strawberries, raspberries and silvanberries)
pure icing (confectioners') sugar, for dusting

TIMELINE

THE DAY BEFORE

Make the meringue cases.

THE DAY OF SERVING

Make the pastry.

Cook the onions.

Prepare the trout.

Prepare the nicoise vegetables.

Hard-boil the eggs.

1—2 HOURS BEFORE SERVING

Assemble the pissaladiere and refrigerate.

Prepare the minted yoghurt and cucumbers.

Boil the potatoes.

Mark the lamb on a grill plate or chargrill pan if cooking in the oven.

Whip the cream.

TO SERVE

Cook the pissaladiere and serve.

Cook the trout.

Arrange either one large nicoise salad on a platter or plate individually.

Place the lamb and potatoes in the oven and serve your nicoise salad.

Put a timer on for the lamb.

Remove the lamb from the oven and rest.

Slice the meat, assemble the lamb platter and serve.

Fill and decorate the vacherin, and serve.

Unlike the other seasons, summer seems to arrive with force. We don't get a gently staggered transition from cooler days to hotter ones – it is suddenly just hot.

Hot weather calls for lazy dining, and lazy dining can call for some lazy cooking. The middle two courses of this menu can be cooked mainly on the barbecue, making it a delicious feast to enjoy on a covered verandah. I often find that the warmth of summer alters the timing of when I want to eat. For instance, I love to start this menu in the late afternoon, kicking off with vermouth on ice and olives, and then gradually wind my way into the evening, serving the remaining courses at leisure.

MENU THREE

MID – LATE SUMMER	*Lunch or Dinner*

Bread *&* olives

Hapuku, tomato *&* zucchini salad

Grilled rump steak *with* salsa agresto,
bearnaise *&* French fries

Almond *&* apricot tart *with* vanilla
& apricot swirl ice cream

Bread & olives

SERVES 8

I take great delight in serving the olives I have brined during the winter in summer. As the supply is limited I like to show them off in splendid isolation, and use bought ones for cooking. If you don't happen to have a stash of home-brined olives, just buy some of your favourite olives from the deli.

1 Baguette (see page 204), thinly sliced
  on the diagonal
extra-virgin olive oil, for brushing
250 g (9 oz) mixed olives

Preheat the barbecue grill plate until hot or heat a chargrill pan over a high heat.

Brush the bread with the oil, then cook on both sides until nice char lines appear.

Serve with a bowl of mixed olives to graze on.

Hapuku, tomato & zucchini salad

SERVES 8

Hapuku is a variety of fish common in southern Australia, New Zealand and Chile (in the northern hemisphere the closest match would be cod). It has good, solid white meat that is best cooked medium–rare and rested. Here, I take it one step further and flake it through a delicious salad.

————————————

Preheat a barbecue grill plate until hot or place a chargrill pan over a high heat. (If you don't have either of these, just use a heavy-based frying pan.)

Preheat the oven to 200°C (400°F).

Toss the garlic and 50 ml (1¾ fl oz) of the oil through the tomatoes. Set aside.

Slice the zucchini very thinly, either with a mandoline or a vegetable peeler. Set aside.

Lightly brush the fish fillet with oil, place on the barbecue or in a chargrill pan and cook until char lines appear. Transfer to a baking tray and bake in the oven for 20 minutes or until the flesh is translucent in the middle. (Alternatively you can lower the hood if you have a hooded barbecue, and cook it for about 15 minutes.) Remove from the oven and leave to cool for 5 minutes.

Flake the fish into the tomato mixture and add the zucchini ribbons, parsley and basil. Dress with the lemon juice and remaining oil, then season to taste with salt and pepper. Serve on a bed of rocket on a large communal plate.

1 garlic clove, crushed
100 ml (3½ fl oz) extra-virgin olive oil
600 g (1 lb 5 oz) mixed cherry and other
*   small tomatoes, halved*
4 yellow and green zucchini (courgettes)
600 g (1 lb 5 oz) hapuku fillet, skin and
*   bones removed*
1 tablespoon chopped flat-leaf
*   (Italian) parsley*
1 tablespoon torn basil
juice of 1 lemon
salt flakes and freshly ground black pepper
100 g (3½ oz) rocket (arugula)

Grilled rump steak *with* salsa agresto, bearnaise & French fries

SERVES 8

Grilled steak is synonymous with hot-weather eating. This recipe is for the whole steak and chips bonanza, but if you don't feel like going to the trouble of chips and bearnaise sauce, make a lovely potato salad and simply serve the steak with the salsa agresto on some rocket. The salsa agresto is a recipe that I learnt from my dear friend Maggie Beer, a woman who loves a summer barbie. It's a delicious paste made with herbs, nuts, oil and verjuice – the consistency reminds me of pesto, but it packs a more interesting punch. When choosing steak, it's best to buy a large, thick piece from a three-year-old steer or from a reasonably marbled piece of wagyu.

_____

To make the bearnaise sauce, melt the butter in a small saucepan, then allow to cool and separate.

Meanwhile, place the shallot, 2 tablespoons water, vinegar and 2 tablespoons of the tarragon in a small saucepan and boil until the liquid has reduced to 1 tablespoon. This should take about 5 minutes.

Place the reduction and egg yolks in a heatproof bowl set over a saucepan of simmering water (make sure the bottom of the bowl does not touch the water). Whisk until the mixture is thick and creamy, then remove from the heat and gradually whisk in the yellow part of the melted butter. Discard the white milk solids. Season the bearnaise sauce to taste and add the remaining tarragon and a squeeze of lemon, if desired. Set aside. This will keep well at room temperature for 2–3 hours, but do not refrigerate.

Meanwhile, preheat the oven to 200°C (400°F).

2 kg (4 lb 6 oz) rump steak, cut into 4 cm (1½ in) thick steaks
salt flakes and freshly ground black pepper
200 g (7 oz) rocket (arugula)
1 quantity French Fries (see page 207)

BEARNAISE SAUCE

300 g (10½ oz) unsalted butter
1 tablespoon chopped French shallot
50 ml (1¾ fl oz) tarragon vinegar or good-quality white wine vinegar
3 tablespoons chopped tarragon
3 egg yolks
salt flakes and freshly ground black pepper
fresh lemon juice, to taste (optional)

SALSA AGRESTO

80 g (2¾ oz) natural almonds
50 g (1¾ oz) walnuts
1 garlic clove
2 handfuls of flat-leaf (Italian) parsley
1 small handful of basil leaves
¾ teaspoon salt flakes
freshly ground black pepper
90 ml (3 fl oz) extra-virgin olive oil
90 ml (3 fl oz) verjuice, plus extra if needed

To make the salsa agresto, spread out the almonds and walnuts on separate baking trays and bake for about 5 minutes, shaking to prevent burning. Remove the nuts from the oven, but leave the oven on. Rub the walnuts in a tea towel to remove the bitter skins, then leave to cool.

Blend the nuts, garlic, parsley, basil, salt and several good grinds of black pepper in a food processor with a little of the oil. With the motor running, slowly add the verjuice and the remaining oil. The consistency should be like pesto – if it needs further thinning, add a bit more verjuice. Try to make this as close to serving as you can as it will start to oxidise if left to sit.

Time to prepare the star of the show: the steaks.

Preheat a barbecue grill plate or chargrill pan until hot.

I always like to start my steak on the grill and finish it in the oven. If you are doing it this way, season the steaks on both sides – you should have two or three thick steaks to cook. Sear the steaks on the grill until nice char lines appear, then place on a baking tray and transfer to the oven. For a medium–rare steak I tend to give it about 5 minutes, then turn over and cook for another 3–5 minutes. Cook it for a bit longer if you prefer it medium or well done.

If you prefer to cook your steaks completely on the barbecue, make sure it is very hot and cook them for about 10 minutes each side.

Rest the steaks on a plate covered loosely with foil.

I like to serve this on a platter in the middle of the table. Scatter the rocket over the platter, then slice the meat against the grain and arrange on the rocket. Spread the salsa agresto across the top in a thick ribbon and serve with the bearnaise sauce and French fries.

Almond & apricot tart *with* vanilla & apricot swirl ice cream

SERVES 8

There is no doubt that for the French the most popular sweet pairing is fruit and pastry. And they are never shy with their ratio of fruit to pastry either – none of this new-age delicate plating here. Apricots, peaches, sour cherries, apples, pears, quinces, prunes – whatever you fancy. Here, in the midst of summer, I fancy apricots, and cut them so they stick up and get a little burnt on the tips to add a pleasant caramelised flavour contrast to the creaminess of the frangipane filling.

This tart is lovely served with a swirl ice cream. If you make apricot jam during the summer, keep the jam you skim off the top during cooking to swirl through ice cream; it's a delicious use of an otherwise wasted product.

———————————

To make the vanilla & apricot swirl ice cream, pour the milk into a saucepan, add the vanilla seeds and bring to scalding point. Whisk the egg yolks and sugar until pale, then pour in the hot milk and whisk until smooth and combined. Return the mixture to the saucepan and cook, stirring, over a medium heat until thickened. Remove from the heat and whisk in the cream. Set aside to cool, then churn in an ice-cream machine according to the manufacturer's instructions. Once churned, swirl the apricot jam through the ice cream and freeze until set.

To make the frangipane, combine the butter and sugar in the bowl of a stand mixer fitted with the paddle attachment and cream until light and fluffy. Add the eggs, one at a time, then add the flour and almond meal and beat until combined. Set aside.

1 quantity Kate's Excellent Shortcrust Pastry
 (see page 208)
500 g (1 lb 2 oz) ripe apricots
pure icing (confectioners') sugar, for dusting

VANILLA & APRICOT SWIRL
 ICE CREAM
500 ml (17 fl oz) milk
½ vanilla bean, split lengthways
 and seeds scraped
6 egg yolks
300 g (10½ oz) caster (superfine) sugar
550 ml (18½ fl oz) pouring
 (single/light) cream
160 g (5½ oz) apricot jam

FRANGIPANE
125 g (4½ oz) unsalted butter, softened
125 g (4½ oz) caster (superfine) sugar
2 eggs
30 g (1 oz) plain (all-purpose) flour
125 g (4½ oz) almond meal

Preheat the oven to 180°C (350°F).

Roll out the pastry on a lightly floured surface to a thickness of 3 mm (⅛ in) and use to line a 24 cm (9½ in) fluted tart tin. Refrigerate while you prepare the apricots.

Cut the apricots in half, then cut each half into thirds. Set aside.

Remove the pastry case from the refrigerator and fill with the frangipane. Push the apricots into the frangipane so they stand with their points up.

Bake for 40 minutes or until a skewer inserted in the centre comes out clean. Remove from the oven and transfer to a wire rack until cool enough to handle, then carefully remove from the tin.

Dust with icing sugar and serve with the vanilla and apricot swirl ice cream.

TIMELINE

2 DAYS AHEAD

If you are making fries, cut them now.

THE DAY BEFORE

Blanch and drain the fries.

Make the base for the ice cream.

THE DAY OF SERVING

Make the pastry.

Make the frangipane.

Roll out the pastry and line the tart case.

Assemble and bake the tart, then cool on a rack (don't refrigerate).

Churn the ice cream.

1—2 HOURS BEFORE SERVING

Prepare the fish.

Get the vegetables ready to go with the fish.

Prepare the steak.

Prepare the rocket.

Make the salsa agresto.

Make the bearnaise sauce.

Preheat the oil for deep-frying and cook the fries.

TO SERVE

Grill the bread.

Serve the bread and olives.

Cook the fish.

Assemble the fish salad and serve.

Cook the steak and rest.

Increase the oil temperature and finish cooking the fries.

Carve the meat, plate and serve.

Present the tart at the table with a bowl of ice cream.

Here in the southern hemisphere, the end of summer heralds Valentine's Day. My farm and restaurant are just up the road from the dramatic Hanging Rock, the setting for the dreamy *Picnic at Hanging Rock*, a film that certainly put 'The Rock', Peter Weir and the Australian film industry on the map. I love a good Valentine's Day menu and, in keeping with the theme, this one is delicate, pretty and romantic.

MENU FOUR

LATE SUMMER	*Lunch or Dinner*

Calamari *with* garlic mayonnaise & zucchini

Quail *with* couscous, rose petals &
cucumber salad

Gateau Saint Honore *with* rose cream

Calamari *with* garlic mayonnaise *&* zucchini

SERVES 8

Succulent calamari, lightly tossed in flour and fried, is one of the great joys in life. It's a lovely sharing dish, and here I serve it with fresh lemon and a crisp 'salad' of zucchini ribbons (yes, I'm still using those summer zucchini whenever I can!). The finishing touch is another example of French farmhouse cookery: persillade, a punchy parsley, lemon and garlic mixture that is quite similar to its Italian cousin, gremolata.

To make the garlic mayonnaise, preheat the oven to 180°C (350°F). Cut the top quarter off the garlic bulb horizontally and discard. Wrap the remainder in foil and roast for 1 hour, then set aside to cool.

Meanwhile, whisk the egg yolks with the vinegar, then gradually drizzle in the grapeseed oil, whisking constantly. Adjust the seasoning with salt, pepper and lemon juice. Remove the garlic from the foil and squeeze out the roasted cloves. Mash together with the mayonnaise and set aside.

To make the persillade, combine the garlic, parsley and lemon zest in a large bowl.

Run the zucchini through a mandoline or shave with a vegetable peeler to make ribbons. Set aside.

Heat 5 cm (2 in) of canola oil in a large heavy-based saucepan to 180°C (350°F) or until a cube of bread dropped in the oil browns in 15 seconds.

4 small green and yellow zucchini (courgettes)
canola oil, for frying
1 kg (2 lb 3 oz) calamari tubes, cleaned and cut into 1 cm (½ in) rings
35 g (1¼ oz) plain (all-purpose) flour
35 g (1¼ oz) cornflour (cornstarch)
¾ teaspoon salt flakes
2 tablespoons olive oil
lemon wedges, to serve

GARLIC MAYONNAISE
1 garlic bulb
6 egg yolks
50 ml (1¾ fl oz) champagne vinegar or white wine vinegar
500 ml (17 fl oz) grapeseed oil
salt flakes and freshly ground black pepper
juice of ½ lemon

PERSILLADE
2 large garlic cloves, crushed
2 tablespoons finely chopped flat-leaf (Italian) parsley
finely grated zest of ¼ lemon

While the oil is heating, place the calamari rings in a large plastic ziplock bag, add the flour, cornflour and salt and shake to coat. Shake off any excess flour, then fry in five or six batches until crisp and just turning golden, about 3 minutes. Make sure the oil comes back up to temperature between each batch. Drain the calamari very quickly on paper towel, then add to the bowl of persillade and toss to coat. If necessary, keep the calamari warm in an oven preheated to 150°C (300°F) while you cook the remaining batches.

Just before serving, toss the zucchini ribbons in the olive oil. Serve the calamari with the roasted garlic mayonnaise, lemon wedges and a pile of dressed zucchini ribbons.

Quail *with* couscous, rose petals *&* cucumber salad

SERVES 8

Little birds and rose petals are a classic combination. This dish has wandered down to the very south of France, seeking a little heat, a little spice from a few Moroccan influences and a lot of romance. It's a beautiful dish to linger over – although you do end up eating with your hands so make sure you serve it with finger bowls and plenty of serviettes.

———————

Remove the backbones from your quail. This is best done by inserting a cook's knife into the cavity of the quail and crunching down on either side of the backbone. Turn the quail over and flatten by pressing forcefully with the palm of your hand.

Combine the rosewater, cumin, cinnamon, lemon juice, salt and pepper and 1 tablespoon of the oil in a large bowl. Add the quail and toss to coat, then set aside to marinate for about 2 hours.

The quail can be cooked in a frying pan, in a chargrill pan or on a barbecue grill plate – it's up to you, just make sure the pan or grill plate is hot. Cook the butterflied quail, skin side down, for 2–3 minutes or until golden, then turn and cook for a further 4–6 minutes until cooked through. (If you have limited space, you can seal the quail in batches on the stovetop, then finish cooking them on a baking tray in a preheated 180°C {350°F} oven for 5 minutes.)

To make the cucumber salad, place the onion, cucumber, lemon juice, oil and chilli in a bowl and gently toss to combine.

To make the couscous, bring 500 ml (17 fl oz) of water to the boil and add a good pinch of salt. Mix in the couscous, then work the butter through gently with a fork. Add the currants and pine nuts and season to taste with salt and pepper. Set aside for 10 minutes, then fluff it up with a fork.

12 quail (this is based on 1½ quail per person; if you're greedy, go for 2 quail each)
1 tablespoon rosewater
3 teaspoons ground cumin
3 teaspoons ground cinnamon
60 ml (2 fl oz) lemon juice
salt flakes and freshly ground black pepper
2 tablespoons olive oil
3 tablespoons crabapple jelly
1 teaspoon white wine vinegar
1 garlic clove, crushed
1 tablespoon finely chopped mint
petals from 2 unsprayed pink or red roses

CUCUMBER SALAD
½ red onion, thinly sliced
4 Lebanese (short) cucumbers
2 teaspoons lemon juice
1 tablespoon olive oil
1 bird's eye chilli, chopped

COUSCOUS
salt flakes and freshly ground black pepper
500 g (1 lb 2 oz) couscous
60 g (2 oz) unsalted butter
75 g (2¾ oz) currants
75 g (2¾ oz) toasted pine nuts

Stir together the jelly, vinegar, garlic and remaining oil in a small saucepan over a low heat for 1–2 minutes to form a fragrant glaze. Stir in the mint.

Spoon the couscous onto a large serving platter and arrange the quail on top. Pour over the glaze, scatter with rose petals and serve the cucumber salad on the side.

Gateau Saint Honore *with* rose cream

SERVES 8

My love of French patisserie has never really diminished. Maybe it's because I enjoy eating late lunches and pastry always seems a better option than a fussy dessert. Or maybe it's just that I'm a sucker for a pretty pastry. This one is traditionally made as a large cake, but in this case I'm bucking against my usual preference for shared food by making it as individual treats – not to be shared, just to be enjoyed.

Roll out the shortcrust pastry on a lightly floured surface to a thickness of 4 mm (³⁄₁₆ in) and cut out ten 8 cm (3¼ in) discs (I always make a couple extra in case of breakages). Place on a plate and refrigerate for at least 20 minutes before baking.

Preheat the oven to 200°C (400°F). Grease and line a large baking tray with baking paper.

Put the discs on the prepared tray, place a sheet of baking paper on top and then another tray to act as a weight. Cook for 15 minutes or until golden brown. Set aside.

Increase the oven temperature to 210°C (410°F) and grease and line another large baking tray with baking paper.

Spoon the choux batter into a piping bag fitted with a 1 cm (½ in) plain nozzle. Pipe 2.5 cm (1 in) rounds onto the prepared tray, leaving 2½ cm (1 in) gaps between each one to allow for spreading (you will need 32 puffs all up, though it's always a good idea to make a few extra). Bake for 10 minutes, then reduce the temperature to 160°C (320°F) and bake for a further 10 minutes. Remove and transfer to a wire rack to cool.

To make the royal icing, lightly whisk the egg white and rose essence in a bowl. Gradually add the icing sugar, whisking until smooth and combined, then tint with the pink food colouring to a soft pink.

1 quantity Kate's Excellent Shortcrust Pastry (see page 208)
1 quantity Choux Pastry (see page 209)
150 ml (5 fl oz) thickened (whipping) cream
1 quantity Pastry Cream (see page 78)
silver dragees, to decorate

ROYAL ICING
1 egg white
½ teaspoon rose essence
240 g (8½ oz) pure icing (confectioners') sugar, sifted
a few drops of pink food colouring

When you are ready to assemble the pastries, whip the cream to stiff peaks, then spoon into a piping bag fitted with a 5 mm (¼ in) closed star nozzle.

Fill the choux puffs with pastry cream. To do this, make a little hole in the bottom of each puff with a small sharp knife. Spoon the pastry cream into a piping bag fitted with a 5 mm (¼ in) plain nozzle (preferably metal) and insert into each hole to fill. Dip the top of each choux puff in the royal icing and decorate with silver dragees.

Place three choux puffs on each pastry disc, 'gluing' them in place with a bit of icing, and place a fourth choux puff on top. Pipe decorative cream details in all the gaps and voila! A pretty little Valentine dessert.

TIMELINE

THE DAY BEFORE

Make the pastry.

Make the choux puffs.

Prepare the pastry cream.

Make the garlic mayonnaise.

Roll and cook the pastry discs.

THE DAY OF SERVING

Clean and slice the calamari, and refrigerate.

Prepare the quail and marinate.

1—2 HOURS BEFORE SERVING

Make the persillade.

Prepare the zucchini.

Toast the nuts for the couscous.

Prepare the cucumber.

Make the royal icing.

Fill the choux puffs with pastry cream, then ice, decorate and set aside somewhere cool.

Whip the cream.

TO SERVE

Heat the oil for the calamari.

Cook and plate the calamari, then serve.

Cook the quail.

Prepare the couscous.

Assemble and serve the quail platter.

Stick the choux puffs to the pastry as directed.

Decorate by filling the spaces with little tufts of cream, then serve and relax.

There are a few basic components to a meal that I feel are a must. Firstly, good bread and butter. Good bread is readily available, but if you feel inspired it really isn't that hard to knock up a couple of very decent baguettes. It's also possible to buy some really glorious butter or, if you leave some cream whisking in a stand mixer long enough, you'll find you've made your own butter! The baguette recipe on page 204 is one I have been using for years, championed by a baker by the name of Richard Bertinet. Don't be shy – it's easy.

I like to serve most main courses with either a simple green salad or a simple green vegetable. It must be those fearsome words still ringing in my ears from childhood: 'eat your greens'. I'm not a big fan of highly complex side dishes. If a side has to be complex, my feeling is that it should get a guernsey on the main team and be a stand-alone course, like a complex salad for example. So a lot of my menus will simply call for a bowl of green vegetables or a green salad. And by the latter I mean beautiful, crisp lettuce leaves, tossed with seasonal herbs, a pinch of salt flakes and a good dose of sherry vinaigrette.

Then there are the potatoes. With a few exceptions I tend to serve my main courses with some form of potato or another. There are so many potato recipes to choose from, so I have whittled them down to those that best complement my menus. To make triple-cooked French fries like we do in restaurants you'll need to start them a couple of days ahead as the potato needs to be soaked and dried before frying. The results are worth it though!

Stocks are one of the backbones of my cooking. A good chicken stock is indispensable for soups, stews and the like, but it is veal stock, and, more importantly, reduced veal stock, that can elevate your food from lovely to sublime. Its incomparable depth of flavour and viscosity add a restaurant-quality flourish to every dish it is used in. Make a batch and freeze it – it is so obliging that, because of its gelatine content, you can freeze it in a block and just cut a bit off when you need it.

And last but not least: pastry. What would a French farmhouse be without a few pastries cooling on the windowsill? Not all home cooks have a patisserie in walking distance so, to recreate the magic, pastry making is a necessary skill to master in the French kitchen. I've included here the four pastries I use most in my cooking.

All the recipes for sides dishes make enough to serve eight people.

BASICS

BAGUETTES

MAKES 4

Mix together the flour and salt in a large bowl.

Tip the dried yeast into the water and stir to dissolve.

Add the water and yeast to the dry ingredients and mix with your fingers or a stout spatula until it comes together in a shaggy mass. Tip the mass onto a lightly floured board or workbench.

Work the dough as follows: put your hands underneath it, lift it, slap it down on the board with a nice satisfying thwack, stretch the top of the dough out in front of you, then fold it back, taking care to do it gently, thus trapping air in between the layers. Do this over and over again (for 3–4 minutes) until the dough starts to form a homogenous smooth mass.

Form the dough into a ball by folding the edges into the centre, pressing down with your thumb, rotating the dough, folding and pressing until you have a neatish ball.

Put the dough back in the mixing bowl, cover with a tea towel and leave to rest somewhere warm and draught-free for about an hour or until doubled in size.

Scrape the rested dough out of the bowl onto a lightly floured surface and cut it into four equal rectangles. Place a floured clean tea towel on the widest baking tray that will fit in your oven. Start with the first piece of dough and cover the others with a tea towel while you work. Pat it out to a 15 × 8 cm (6 × 3¼ in) rectangle. Fold the top half into the middle, and then fold the bottom half into the middle, pressing each seam with your fingers, then fold the top to the bottom and push those edges together.

500 g (1 lb 2 oz) white strong flour
10 g (¼ oz) fine sea salt
10 g (¼ oz) instant dried yeast
350 g (12 oz) lukewarm water (in this case you must weigh it, don't just pour it into a measuring jug)

Now, pick up the dough and place it seam side down, pat out to a 20 × 10 cm (8 × 4 in) rectangle and repeat this process. This is called giving the baguette a spine. Once repeated, roll the dough between your hands, making points at each end and place it on the floured tea towel.

Repeat with the remaining portions of dough, bunching up the tea towel to create a barrier between each baguette so they don't stick together while proving. Cover the tray with a clean tea towel and leave the dough to prove in a warm place for 30 minutes.

Preheat the oven to 240°C (475°F).

While the bread is proving, put a roasting tin in the bottom of the oven and bring a kettle of water to the boil.

When you are ready to bake, roll the baguettes gently onto a workbench and remove the tea towel. Lightly dust the tray. Use a sharp knife to slash the tops diagonally three to five times, then gently return to the tray. Open the oven and slide in the tray, then pour the boiling water into the roasting tin at the bottom and close the door.

Bake for about 20 minutes or until golden and cooked through. Cool on a wire rack.

Just a side note, if you're not keen on the whole bread-baking business, this dough makes an absolutely ripper flatbread. Make the dough as above, then prove, cut into eight and roll into flat discs. Lightly oil the dough and grill in a very hot chargrill pan on both sides. It's delicious.

GREENS

BLANCHED GREEN BEANS

750 g (1 lb 11 oz) green beans, topped and tailed

Cook the beans in a saucepan of salted boiling water for 5 minutes. Drain.

BLANCHED BRUSSELS SPROUTS

750 g (1 lb 11 oz) brussels sprouts, trimmed, outer leaves removed

Place the sprouts in a saucepan of salted boiling water and cook for 5–7 minutes or until just tender. Drain.

BLANCHED BROCCOLINI

750 g (1 lb 11 oz) broccolini

Cut about 5–7.5 cm (2–3 in) off the bottom of the broccolini. Place in a saucepan of salted boiling water and cook for 5–7 minutes or until just tender. Drain.

KALES WITH GARLIC

1 bunch cavolo nero
1 bunch curly kale
2 tablespoons olive oil
1 garlic clove, thinly sliced
salt flakes and freshly ground black pepper

Strip the leaves from the stems of the cavolo nero and kale, then roughly chop. Blanch the greens in a large saucepan of boiling water for 2–3 minutes.

Meanwhile, warm the oil in a large frying pan over a low heat, add the garlic and cook gently until softened. Increase the heat to high. Drain the greens and toss in the garlicky oil, then season and serve.

POTATOES

MASHED POTATO

1 kg (2 lb 3 oz) all-purpose potatoes (such as desiree or pontiac)
100 g (3½ oz) unsalted butter, cut into cubes
180–310 ml (6–10½ fl oz) pouring (single/light) cream, brought to the boil and kept hot
salt flakes

Put the whole, unpeeled potatoes in a saucepan of cold water, bring to the boil and cook until a fork inserted meets barely any resistance. This will likely take 30 minutes or more. Peel the potatoes while they are still hot, then pass them through a mouli or mash them by hand with a potato masher.

Add the butter and stir vigorously until melted and incorporated. Pour in 180 ml (6 fl oz) of the hot cream in a slow stream, whipping constantly with a wooden spoon to incorporate air into the mixture. Season with salt, then add more cream if needed to reach the desired consistency. For that extra level of refinement, pass the puree through a drum sieve.

ROASTED DUCK FAT POTATOES

1.5 kg (3 lb 5 oz) Dutch cream or nicola potatoes
100 g (3½ oz) duck fat (always worth having some of this in your refrigerator)
salt flakes
chopped flat-leaf (Italian) parsley and crushed garlic, to serve (optional)

Preheat the oven to 210°C (410°F).

Peel the potatoes and cut them into 4 cm (1½ in) pieces.

Place the duck fat in a roasting tin that will accommodate the potatoes in a single layer. Heat the tin and fat in the oven for 5 minutes. Carefully add the potatoes, season with a sprinkling of salt, then roast for 25 minutes.

Reduce the temperature to 180°C (350°F) and roast for a further 15 minutes or until golden and cooked through. Give them a little shake every 15 minutes or so during cooking, and if they stick to the pan, loosen them with a spatula.

These are lovely just as they are, but are also delicious finished with parsley and crushed garlic at the very end.

CREAMED POTATOES

1.5 kg (3 lb 5 oz) good-quality all-purpose potatoes
  (such as desiree)
1 small garlic clove, crushed
salt flakes and freshly ground black pepper
600 ml (20½ fl oz) pouring (single/light) cream
50 g (1¾ oz) unsalted butter
freshly grated nutmeg

Preheat the oven to 190°C (375°F).

Peel the potatoes and thinly slice them. Wash the slices well in cold water to removes any excess starch, then pat dry with paper towel. Place in a bowl and toss with the garlic and a sprinkling of salt and pepper.

Transfer to a large baking dish and spread them out evenly. Pour over the cream, then dot with butter and grate a little nutmeg over the top. Bake for 1–1¼ hours or until the potato is tender.

FRENCH FRIES

1.5 kg (3 lb 5 oz) very large sebago or nicola potatoes
  (the largest you can find)
vegetable oil, for deep-frying
salt flakes

Peel the potatoes, cut them into shape and soak them in cold water in the refrigerator overnight.

Drain the cut potatoes, then place in a large saucepan and cover with water. Bring to the boil, then reduce the heat and simmer for 8 minutes or until just tender. Drain carefully, then spread them out on a tray and refrigerate overnight to dry out.

Heat the oil in a large heavy-based saucepan or deep-fryer to 130°C (250°F) or until a cube of bread dropped in the oil browns in 45 seconds. Cook the chips for 8 minutes, then drain very well.

Shortly before you are ready to serve, increase the temperature of the oil to 185°C (360°F) or until a cube of bread browns in 10 seconds and cook the chips for 3–5 minutes or until golden brown. Drain well and season with salt.

STOCKS

VEAL STOCK

2 kg (4 lb 6 oz) veal bones
3 carrots, cut into 8 cm (3¼ in) pieces
3 sticks celery, cut into 8 cm (3¼ in) pieces
3 onions, quartered
1 bay leaf
3 thyme sprigs
6 stalks flat-leaf (Italian) parsley
1 leek top (optional)

To make the veal stock, put the bones in a 10–15 litre (350–500 fl oz) stockpot, cover with cold water and bring to the boil. Skim the surface to remove any impurities. Add the vegetables and herbs and return to the boil, then skim again, reduce the heat and simmer for 8 hours, skimming occasionally. Strain, discarding the solids. This is now ready to use in any recipes calling for veal stock. The stock will keep in the refrigerator for a week, or will freeze happily. Makes about 2½ litres (85 fl oz).

To make reduced veal stock, boil the stock for about 2 hours or until reduced by three-quarters – you will be left with a dark brown, unctuous liquid. This can be frozen in a block and cut when required, or frozen in ice-block trays. It will keep in the refrigerator for up to 10 days. Makes about 650 ml (22½ fl oz) of pure magic.

CHICKEN STOCK

2 kg (4 lb 6 oz) chicken bones
2 carrots, cut into 4 cm (1½ in) pieces
4 sticks celery, cut into 4 cm (1½ in) pieces
2 onions, quartered
1 bay leaf
3 thyme sprigs
6 stalks flat-leaf (Italian) parsley
1 leek top (optional)

Put the bones in a 7½–10 litre (250–350 fl oz) stockpot, cover with cold water and bring to the boil. Skim the surface to remove any impurities. Add the vegetables and herbs and return to the boil, then skim again, reduce the heat and simmer for 4 hours, skimming occasionally. Strain, discarding the solids. The stock will keep in the refrigerator for a week, or will freeze well. Makes about 5 litres (170 fl oz).

PASTRY

KATE'S EXCELLENT SHORTCRUST PASTRY

125 g (4½ oz) unsalted butter, cut into small cubes
210 g (7½ oz) plain (all-purpose) flour
salt flakes
1 egg

Work the butter and a pinch of salt through the flour until it resembles coarse breadcrumbs. Make a well in the centre, add the egg and 25 ml (¾ fl oz) cold water and bring together into a dough – try not to handle it too much or the pastry will be tough. Wrap in plastic wrap and chill for 30 minutes before using.

I prefer to make and roll pastry on the day I want to serve it, but you can make it a day ahead and keep it in the refrigerator overnight, if you like.

PUFF PASTRY

500 g (1 lb 2 oz) plain (all-purpose) flour,
 plus extra for dusting
salt flakes
juice of ½ lemon, strained
500 g (1 lb 2 oz) cold unsalted butter

Mix together the flour, a pinch of salt, 300 ml (10½ fl oz) water and lemon juice in a bowl to form a dough. Turn out onto a lightly floured surface and knead quickly until a little elastic. Place on a plate, then cover and refrigerate overnight.

Bash the cold butter with a rolling pin into a 24 × 12 cm (9½ × 4½ in) rectangle. This helps to make the butter pliable without heating it too much. Roll the dough on a lightly floured surface into a 36 × 12 cm (14¼ × 4½ in) rectangle. Place the sheet of butter at one end – there should be one-third of the pastry not covered by butter. Fold this part in and then fold the remaining (buttered) third over, a bit like folding a letter into three. Rotate the dough so that an open end is facing you and roll a little with a rolling pin to distribute the butter into the corners. Seal each end with your fingers to keep the butter enclosed.

Begin the first of four 'turns'. Dust your rolling surface with flour. Roll the pastry into a 36 × 12 cm (14¼ × 4½ in) rectangle, then fold one end into the middle and repeat with the other end. Close the two ends together, like closing a book (not surprisingly, this is called a book turn). Wrap the dough in plastic wrap or foil and refrigerate for 30 minutes. Repeat this process three more times until you have made four book turns. The pastry will become increasingly delicate after each turn, so make sure your bench is well floured. After the final turn, it's best to rest the pastry for an hour or more before rolling and cutting.

CHOUX PASTRY

100 g (3½ oz) chopped unsalted butter
salt flakes
140 g (5 oz) plain (all-purpose) flour
4 eggs

Preheat the oven to 210°C (410°F).

Combine the butter, 250 ml (8½ fl oz) of cold water and a pinch of salt in a saucepan set over a medium heat and stir until the butter has melted. Bring to the boil, then add the flour and stir over a low heat until the pastry forms a ball and comes away from the side of the pan. Transfer the dough to the bowl of a stand mixer fitted with the paddle attachment and allow to cool for a few minutes. Add the eggs one by one, mixing thoroughly after each addition. (If you don't have a stand mixer, just put the dough in a mixing bowl and beat in the eggs with a wooden spoon.)

The pastry is now ready to be spooned into a piping bag, piped and baked. Bake the choux in the preheated oven for 10 minutes, then reduce the oven temperature to 160°C (320°F) and cook for another 10–15 minutes until the choux is crisp and golden.

SWEET SHORTCRUST PASTRY

400 g (14 oz) plain (all-purpose) flour
100 g (3½ oz) caster (superfine) sugar
200 g (7 oz) unsalted butter, cut into small cubes
1 egg yolk

Place the flour, sugar and butter in a food processor and blitz until it resembles breadcrumbs. Add the egg yolk and 60 ml (2 fl oz) of cold water and mix until the dough forms a ball. Remove, gently pat into a disc and refrigerate for 1 hour before using.

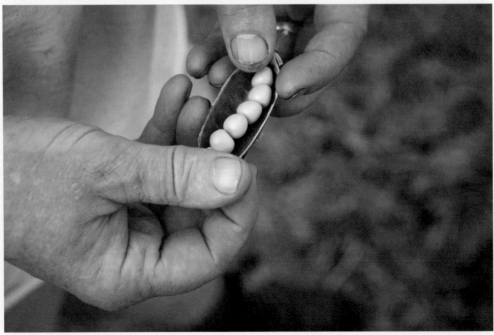

ACKNOWLEDGEMENTS

ANNIE SMITHERS

What a wonderful experience it has been to collaborate with the immensely talented Robin Cowcher. Thank you, Robin, for taking such care in illustrating my world so incredibly carefully and accurately. You have caught the sense of whimsy that pervades my life on every page.

To the team at Hardie Grant, especially Jane Willson, thank you for believing in such a work and allowing it to come to life. Thank you to Andy Warren for your beautiful sense of design, and to Andrea O'Connor for making sure I stay on the right track.

To my editor, Rachel Carter, once again you have untangled my words into proper English without me ever feeling that I didn't write it all correctly in the first place. You are a true marvel.

To Patricia Niven, friend and photographer, thank you for coming so far to take such lovely images.

To two women who loom large in my life, in both friendship and mentoring, Stephanie Alexander and Kate Hill, thank you both for all you have taught me and for all the inspiration, and for your friendship.

To all my delightful restaurant customers who have enjoyed many of these menus, thank you for your continued support and appreciation of what we do at du Fermier. To my friends, especially the ever-charming and supportive Charmaine and the generosity of the Meirelles'.

And to the lovely Susan, thank you for steering me safely through this journey.

ROBIN COWCHER

It has been a joy to get to know Annie Smithers through the drawings for this book. Thank you Annie for sharing your world, your generosity of spirit and for your faith in my work. The pictures, feelings and flavours you create with your home, du Fermier and household menagerie were an inspiration and a pleasure to paint. Special mention to Kitten, Fenn and Tommy!

To Jane Willson and Hardie Grant, thank you for the opportunity to collaborate with Annie and for allowing me a free rein creatively. Your belief in this book and my contribution to it was and is invaluable.

To Andrea O'Connor, your timely direction and thoughtful feedback was much appreciated.

To Andy Warren, thank you for your superb design and your sensitive art direction, also for your patience and care throughout.

Thank you to my parents, Mardi and Bruce Cowcher, for early encouragement to draw and for giving me a lifelong love of gardens, cooking and animals. And to those good friends and family who offered advice and support along the way, heartfelt thanks.

INDEX

Published in 2017 by Hardie Grant Books, an imprint of Hardie Grant Publishing

Hardie Grant Books (Melbourne)
Building 1, 658 Church Street
Richmond, Victoria 3121
hardiegrantbooks.com.au

Hardie Grant Books (London)
5th & 6th Floors
52–54 Southwark Street
London SE1 1UN
hardiegrantbooks.co.uk

A Cataloguing-in-Publication entry is available from the catalogue of the National Library of Australia
     at www.nla.gov.au

Annie's Farmhouse Kitchen
978 1 74379 264 3

Publishing Director: Jane Willson
Managing Editor: Marg Bowman
Project Editor: Andrea O'Connor
Editor: Rachel Carter
Design Manager: Mark Campbell
Designer: Andy Warren
Photographer: Patricia Niven
Illustrator: Robin Cowcher
Production Manager: Todd Rechner

Colour reproduction by Splitting Image Colour Studio
Printed in China by 1010 Printing International Limited